YOUR STORY HAS A VILLAIN

YOUR STORY HAS A VILLAIN

IDENTIFY SPIRITUAL WARFARE AND LEARN HOW TO DEFEAT THE ENEMY

JONATHAN POKLUDA

WITH JON GREEN

W Publishing Group

AN IMPRINT OF THOMAS NELSON

Published in Nashville, Tennessee, by W Publishing, an imprint of Thomas Nelson.

Thomas Nelson titles may be purchased in bulk for educational, business, fundraising, or sales promotional use. For information, please email SpecialMarkets@ThomasNelson.com.

Scripture quotations are taken from the Holy Bible, New International Version®, NIV®. Copyright © 1973, 1978, 1984, 2011 by Biblica, Inc.® Used by permission of Zondervan. All rights reserved worldwide. www.zondervan.com. The "NIV" and "New International Version" are trademarks registered in the United States Patent and Trademark Office by Biblica, Inc.®

Any internet addresses, phone numbers, or company or product information printed in this book are offered as a resource and are not intended in any way to be or to imply an endorsement by Thomas Nelson, nor does Thomas Nelson vouch for the existence, content, or services of these sites, phone numbers, companies, or products beyond the life of this book.

ISBN 978-1-4003-4117-7 (TP)
ISBN 978-1-4003-4120-7 (audiobook)
ISBN 978-1-4003-4119-1 (ePub)

Library of Congress Control Number: 9781400341177

Printed in the United States of America

24 25 26 27 28 LBC 5 4 3 2 1

Dear reader,

Would you please pray for God to always protect my marriage to Monica and our children, Presley, Finley, and Weston?

Thank you!

JP

CONTENTS

PART 3: HOW TO FIGHT BACK

FOREWORD

AS A CHILD, I REMEMBER HEARING A STORY ABOUT a frog that was put in a pot of water on a stove. I always wondered what that frog did to get placed in the pot, but I've never heard a solid explanation for it. You're probably familiar with the story as well. In cool water, all is well for the frog, and it feels happy, safe, and secure. When the stove is turned on, the frog never realizes the water is getting hotter, and as the temperature increases, so does the frog's tolerance for its personal Jacuzzi. Eventually, bubbles start popping and the frog is boiled alive. Tragic story, truly.

This tale is connected to a nineteenth century science experiment that is now debated. However, it still works as an excellent metaphor for the people of God and how we view and relate to the reality of the spiritual realm.[1] My fear is that we have become the proverbial "frog in the pot of water." We've grown complacent to the spiritual climate around us and simply become accustomed to the spiritual temperature gradually increasing around us. The outcome is a disaster, because we are left vulnerable.

Vulnerability is the perfect place for deception. The truth is, we have an age-old enemy whose singular purpose is to derail us from our relationship with God through distraction. In other words, every one of our stories has a villain, and it is imperative that we recognize the Villain for who he is, how he works, and what our response ought to be.

Some may wonder: *Why should we even care about the spiritual realm?*

This was the very question I asked before starting a six-year journey writing a PhD dissertation covering this very topic. My doctoral advisor, the late Dr. Michael Heiser, once said to me, "What parts of the Bible aren't supernatural?" After reflecting on his question, I came up with my own question I ask whenever lecturing or teaching on the subject. And so, I pose it to you today:

What part of the following statement summarizing the core of what we believe as Christians is *not* supernatural in nature?

> We believe that Jesus is the Son of God, fully God and fully man, that he left heaven, entered earth through immaculate conception, lived a perfect human life, died on a literal cross, physically rose on the third day and defeated death through death, and now sits at the right hand of the Father.

Answer: Not a single part.

And yet, while the story of Jesus is filled with awe, wonder, and the supernatural, there is always a counterfeit story trying to undermine the story of Christ. This is not by coincidence. It is intentional. This is exactly why 1 Peter 5:8 calls us to "be sober-minded, be alert. Your adversary the devil is prowling around like a roaring lion, looking for anyone he can devour." Peter uses the Greek word nēphō, which we translate in English as "sober" and is the opposite of intoxication. Paul uses the Greek word methē, meaning "intoxication" in two vice lists connecting it to the works of darkness (Romans 13:13; Galatians 5:21).[2]

In other words, Peter calls us to have total clarity of mind because Paul reminds us of the very real presence of dark forces.[3]

Why is clarity of mind so important? Because Peter straight up lets us know that we have an enemy, and he wants to lead us into compromise (this is what intoxication does) in mind, spirit, and emotion so that he can pounce and take us out.

We need both wisdom to see these schemes and the Holy Spirit to stand against them.

What you will find in these pages is wisdom that comes from above (James 3:17), so we can be fully aware, with sobriety of mind, of the counterfeit wisdom that comes from below. I can think of no one better to write this book and be our guide than my friend, JP.

One of the big questions of our age is the question of truth. There is "The Truth" (from above) and then, there is counterfeit truth presented to us as beautiful but deceptively destructive (from below). One of the things I admire about JP is how every Friday he faithfully answers countless questions as they relate to the Christian life, always pointing us to The Truth found in Jesus.

JP's Friday Q&A responses are precise, pastoral, and always to the point. And this book, *Your Story Has a Villain*, is no exception. It is theologically precise. It is pastorally caring. And it is refreshingly to the point. And most of all, it powerfully leads us to the hero of our story, Jesus the risen Christ and King of the Cosmos.

Joel Muddamalle, PhD
Theologian In Residence,
Proverbs 31 Ministries

Author of *The Hidden
Peace: Finding True Security,
Strength, and Confidence
Through Humility*

PROLOGUE

A Villain's Letter

OCTOBER 16, 2019

Dear Abaddon,

I'm writing to share some exciting developments from our latest meeting, chaired by none other than the chief villain himself, Lucifer. The gathering was an impressive sight, with thousands of our kind, each more menacing than the last.

The chief villain himself, a figure both terrifying and magnetic, revealed the results of his simple yet potent plan: *"Divide them!"* He crafted a new scheme, not through brute force, but through a worldwide pandemic. This isn't just about causing death; it's about creating discord.

The pandemic strategy was to use the fear and uncertainty of this disease to turn people against each other. He wants chaos in families, communities, and even within their faith. He wants arguing over masks, vaccines, and whom to trust, completely losing sight of their usual togetherness.

Take, for instance, an awful human named David. We

are sick of his disgusting acts of generosity. The virus struck his parents, transforming them from sources of solace to symbols of fear. His father's sudden death amid this chaos caused a rift of emotional and physical distance—exactly what we aim for.

Our goal, Abaddon, is crystal clear. Our goal is to exploit global crises to instill doubt and fear. Let them all question their so-called benevolent Creator. Push them toward harmful coping mechanisms and erode their faith. Take any chance to draw more humans away from the path of righteousness.

Remember, our triumph isn't just in their suffering and loss, but in leading them to question and abandon their Maker. We must disrupt their joy, unity, and hope. This is our chance to destroy them all, or said better, watch them destroy each other.

Stay sharp and cunning,

Molech

INTRODUCTION

The Villain Is Here

IF THE DEVIL WERE GOING TO TAKE YOU OUT, HOW would he do it?

Would it be lust leading to an affair? Would it be greed, leading you to cut corners to get ahead? Would it be pride, so you become so self-reliant that you push away those who love you most?

Or maybe the Enemy would play head games with you. Maybe he would get you thinking about all you don't have, while comparing yourself to others. Maybe he would send you into a deep, dark depression, or cause you to be an anxious, overcontrolling mess.

How would the Evil One ruin you? I find it interesting that we believe there is a world full of dark opposition, and we're content knowing very little about it or how it works. So take a minute to answer this question. I'd be curious to know how your answer changes by the time you finish this book.

NUMB TO THE REALITY

Before you read any further, we should start this off with a confession. Why not, right?

I had not paid much attention to spiritual warfare for a large portion of my adult life. Honestly, it rarely even crossed my mind. I was almost forty, had grown up in the church (multiple, actually), came to an authentic faith in Jesus in my twenties, and had been in vocational ministry (i.e., a pastor) for almost fifteen years. A natural assumption would be that I never *stopped* thinking about spiritual warfare, but somehow over time the opposite had become true.

When I was younger, the reality of a spiritual war unfolding in real time was ingrained into me. I grew up in a small town in South Texas called Cuero. Our high school mascot was the Gobblers. Yes, like a turkey (which doesn't really have anything to do with this story, it just felt like something you should know).

Growing up in what you might call a religiously eclectic family was interesting and, at times, confusing. My dad was Catholic, my mom was Lutheran, and I ended up spending a lot of time at both of their churches. I also attended the local Catholic school in my elementary and middle school years. When I was in religion class, I have this distinct memory of sitting in my cramped school desk and being taught that there were angels and demons fighting all around us at any given time, even though we couldn't see them. As my classmates sat there daydreaming about who knows what, I remember thinking, *Wait, is this real?*

If I close my eyes, I can picture St. Michael's Catholic Church in that small town. As you walk into the sanctuary, the first things you see are ornate statues all around the room. There is a crucifix of Jesus to the left. There is an enormous marble altar, and right behind that is a golden tabernacle where (under lock and key) the gold cup and the chalice used for Communion are stored. Right above that, squarely in the center of the room, is an elaborate statue of Michael the archangel stabbing a dragonlike creature with a spear. Sunday after Sunday, sitting on those hard, wooden pews, gave me imagery of what might be going on in the spiritual world. But is that what it really looks like?

I also remember being at my grandmother Honey's house, which was in an even smaller town a short drive away from where we lived. Her TV was always set to those free Christian channels you could get on basic cable back in the 1980s. All of Honey's favorite televangelists were on there, and she watched them religiously (no pun intended). She also had a video of a documentary about satanism and the occult (although I am still not sure why). This movie was dark—and I mean *dark*.

When I was eight years old, I started watching it when I would go to her house. It was terrifying and interesting all at the same time. For a kid who was not allowed to watch horror movies, this was quite a loophole that I found. But it was in no way good for my soul, considering decades have passed and I can still picture some of the scenes in my mind today.

This interest in darkness continued throughout my childhood. Art was my "thing." I loved to draw, and it was what I was best at. But unlike most kids who drew portraits of their houses or their families or their favorite athletes, my drawings were . . . different. They were darker. As I sat and scribbled away in my journals and those cheap spiral-bound school notebooks, I drew skulls, fangs, blood—there were clearly some dark influences.

Before you feel the need to stage an intervention for the pre-teen version of me, my interests changed over time. I started paying attention to different things, and my interest in darkness became merely background noise as I grew older. I discovered the world (the actual world, not the spiritual world) and all it had to offer. It was all-consuming trying to fit in, experiencing pleasure, and chasing everything money could buy. I still prayed when I remembered to and wore a cross necklace from time to time, but that was the extent to which I cared about the spiritual realm.

Fast-forward to my early twenties, and I came to faith in a real way sitting in the back row of a church in Dallas, still hungover from the night before. All of a sudden, my heart started to change. I was surrounded by other believers who were sharpening me and pushing me to look more like Christ. Some of the sin strongholds that had gripped my life for a decade started to loosen, and habitual sin patterns I never thought I would be free from almost vanished overnight.

Eventually, I started working at a church. Me, the same guy who was fascinated by a satanism documentary as a kid, got hired by a church! I coordinated small groups; I started speaking to young adults; and I even got to speak on the stage in big church. (Side note: Why do we all feel the need to call it big church, even into adulthood?)

Jesus changed my life. I was growing in spiritual maturity, in my knowledge and understanding of God's Word, and I had the privilege of calling others to do the same. But something strange happened: Even as a devoted follower of Christ, my awareness of this invisible, intangible spiritual battle we are all in stayed in the background. Somehow, even as a full-time employee of a church, I was less aware of that part of the spiritual realm than I had been as a young boy.

THE MACRO AND MICRO

We all have areas of our lives where we become fixated on the microdetails, but not the macro, big-picture parts of certain subjects. I could get deep into the weeds with you on how to plan an outstanding vacation to Mexico, how to buy the right golf cart at a low price, and how the Bible fits together as one cohesive story even though it is made up of sixty-six books written by about forty different authors. Why? Because I have spent time researching, studying, and trying to master these subjects to the best of my abilities.

We accept other realities without understanding them at a big-picture level. I know that in the United States we have three branches of government. I can tell you who the current president is. But you could quickly call my bluff if you asked me how a bill becomes a law or who the twenty-seventh president was (William Howard Taft—I looked it up so you wouldn't have to). Somewhere along the way in my walk with Jesus, I reached a point where I had grown content in my big-picture grasp on the spiritual world.

Now, don't get me wrong: I had a baseline understanding of what was going on in the world. I knew God has an Enemy (whom Christians most often refer to as Satan) and I knew it was that Enemy's job to disrupt and destroy the perfect world God had made. I knew that because of that Enemy, sin existed, and sin was what keeps us away from an eternity with God forever. I knew God sent His Son, Jesus, to earth to live a sinless life, to be crucified on the cross, and to be resurrected three days later for the forgiveness of our sins. I knew the facts. I believed (and still believe) all those statements are true.

What I rarely thought about, though, was how all of that played out in the day-to-day of real life. When my car wouldn't start and I was late for a meeting, was that spiritual warfare? Or was it just a bad spark plug? Could it be both? How? When I went through a season of intense anxiety in 2017, was that some kind of attack? Or was that simply a stressful season at work and all that comes with marriage and raising three young children? When I would see horrific stories in the news, were those people possessed by demons? Or were those stories the result of people making terrible choices? So many questions, but too few answers.

So, what changed? In short, I moved to a new city and started a new job. In January 2019, our family sold our house in Dallas, packed up our belongings, and moved to Waco so I could be the lead pastor of a church there that we believed God was calling our family to. Immediately upon arriving in Waco, I felt a sense of spiritual darkness in the city that I could not quite place my finger on. In a city with one of the world's largest Baptist universities and almost 100 Baptist churches alone (not including every other denomination and nondenominational churches), that feels like a weird thing to say.

Waco has a complicated history. It is an amazing place with amazing people, but it has been part of a spiritual tug-of-war for a couple of centuries. It has long been home to Baylor University, a prominent Baptist university, but it was also home to one of the last remaining red-light districts in Texas and the infamous David Koresh–led Branch Davidian compound on the outskirts of the city. There was seemingly a church on every corner, but it was also home to a horrific public lynching in 1916.[1]

Fast-forward to the twenty-first century, and the tug-of-war was continuing. I was experiencing a facade of religiosity and cultural Christianity in a whole new way. And I could not shake that feeling that there was something spiritually oppressive happening in my new city—a city I loved and was committed to ministering in. I started bringing it up in our staff meetings and mentioning it on stage in sermons.

People always wanted me to unpack that and explain what I meant, but I couldn't quite put it into words for a couple of years. I was reading, learning, listening, and discussing it with people around me. A couple of years later, we decided to devote a sermon series to spiritual warfare, and that is when my awareness of the unseen reached a whole new level.

WHAT I KNOW TO BE TRUE

The more I've thought about it, the more I am convinced that the question we (meaning the church—all followers of Jesus) should be asking is, *How did we get like this? How did we become so unaware of the spiritual battle we are in the midst of?* I am going to go out on a limb and assume something here: You and I are not all that different. If you are a Christian, you are most likely not very aware of the spiritual war that is being waged around you at this exact moment as you flip through these pages. Why is our default posture to let the spiritual realm become the background noise of our lives as we go about our days, weeks, months, and years?

Far too many of us confine our interaction with the spiritual realm to a seventy-five-minute church service (or ninety minutes if your pastor's sermon runs long) once a week. Maybe you are even part of a small group or are serving the local church throughout the week using the gifts and abilities God has given you. Maybe you spend time daily reading your Bible and talking with God in prayer. All those things are great, and those disciplines will hopefully grow your love and affection for Jesus. Keep going! But if that's the extent of our spiritual lives, we are still missing out on something important.

Here's what I want to make abundantly clear: Your story has a villain. You most likely don't think about him much, but he thinks of you every single day. He has an active plot to bring you pain and suffering. He wants to drive you to despair. When you are scrolling through social media comparing your life to others, he is involved. When you want to buy something you hope will make you happy, he is involved. And sometimes the "he" is actually "they." They team up when they need to. You are at war.

It's important to note that when we talk about the villain or the

Enemy in this book, that is a term that will be used interchangeably at different points to talk about Satan and his demonic forces. In an often-referenced verse, John 10:10, Jesus describes the Enemy as a thief who "comes only to steal and kill and destroy." If we pause to look at the world (and even within our churches), we can see this is happening all around us. Scroll through social media, flip through the channels, or glance at your favorite news app to see all the ways this is taking place.

We often fail to think about the second half of that verse. Jesus shows us the alternative to the thief by saying that He has come so we "may have life, and have it to the full." I believe there is a full, abundant, joyful, good life available to all who follow Jesus, but too few of us actually experience that life here on earth. We experience the thief robbing us in our spiritual lives. We fall prey to the villain's tactics and end up discouraged and downtrodden—which is exactly what he wants.

WHERE WE ARE HEADED

It's important that you know this up front: I do not have special letters behind my name. I didn't get a PhD in demonology. There are people far, far more intelligent than me who have written entire books and devoted their entire careers to some of the things we will talk about in the pages ahead. But I am a pastor. I have been for a couple of decades now. I have seen thousands and thousands of case studies. Perhaps the most important skill in ministry is pattern recognition. With every single person I have interacted with over the last two decades, one pattern has emerged: there is a villain, and he's seeking to rob people of a life with Jesus.

I'm going to make another assumption: We all want to live that full life that Jesus is talking about. No one reading this is thinking, *I really hope to live a mediocre existence until I get to go be with Jesus in eternity.* But to get to the result we are all hoping for, we are going to have to reverse engineer this problem. If we want to live a full life as a devoted follower of Jesus, what (or more accurately, *who*) is going to prevent that from happening?

This book is broken up into three parts:

- Who the villain is
- What the villain does
- How to fight back

I pray that the stories you will read, the scriptures you will encounter, and the things you learn will bring you to a greater awareness and understanding of what is going on all around us. My life is different now than it was a few years ago because of what I have learned. If we understand our Enemy's tactics and endgame, we stand a much better chance of defeating him.

Let's learn all we can.

PART 1

WHO THE
VILLAIN IS

I'M A SUCKER FOR WAR MOVIES—ALWAYS HAVE
been. I think it is, in part, because my most formative years happened to be during the golden age of war movies and shows.
Hacksaw Ridge is one of my favorites. Now, there is a lot of violence
throughout the film (it's a war movie, after all), so I'm not going
to say, "Go watch it immediately." But I think it's a great movie.
If you've never seen it before, the movie is split into two different
kinds of scenes, and the story bounces back and forth between
when the main character is at home and when he is at war.

When he is home, he is pursuing a young woman. The sky is
blue, the grass is green, the birds are chirping, and it is this really
sweet love story of a young couple. In the very next scene, he is off
at war. He is a medic in the military, so it's his job to go out onto the
battlefield and look for wounded soldiers he can bring back to help.
It's dark. It's smoky. The sky is gray; there are bullets whizzing by
and grenades going off. At no point during the movie are you, the
viewer, ever confused about whether he is at home or at war.

One of the starkest realities of war for the deployed is that it is *always* happening. You are never debating with your buddies if the war is still going on or if it is over. You could be eating lunch one minute and then something happens nearby, and all of a sudden your helmet is back on and you are in the Humvee ready to go. Your brain is so conditioned to always be "on" that it is difficult to relax and turn off that feeling, even once the war is over and you have returned home. War does not follow a nine-to-five, Monday-through-Friday schedule. Fighting could break out at any time, and no one is more aware of that than the people actually fighting in the war.

What if I told you the Enemy's greatest tactic against modern-day Christians is to lull you into thinking there is not a war going on? We do not even realize Satan and his army are actively trying to take us down. For far too many of us, Sunday morning is the only time we stop to ask the question, "Is the war still going on?" We have fallen right into the trap set by the Enemy when we lose sight of the fact that we are in a war right now.

You see, I believe we are either oblivious to or have grown numb to some significant realities over time. We have fallen into the trap of believing that this world is our home, when the New Testament makes it clear time and time again that we are to be citizens of a different kingdom (Ephesians 2:19; Philippians 3:20).

It's important for us to go back and build upon the basics of our faith. We need to revisit some foundational truths of Scripture and make sure we understand what the Bible says about spiritual warfare. I was talking with a friend of mine and he said, "I think the reason we don't think or talk about spiritual warfare all that much is because the Bible doesn't say much about it."

I pushed back and said, "The Bible talks more about spiritual warfare than it does marriage." Think about that! There are so many topics we think about and discuss in church that are backed by biblical principles but not directly addressed, like how we should date and what jobs we should (or shouldn't) take. But spiritual warfare is mentioned throughout the Bible! Scripture has a lot to say about the reality that the villain is out to rob us, presenting the topic both descriptively ("here is what is happening in this story") and prescriptively ("here is what you should do"). The problem is that the Bible talks a lot more about spiritual warfare than our churches do, so many modern-day Christians have a huge theological gap in their knowledge.

Think about Christianity as a house, with all your different theologies (what you believe about God) as the different rooms. On the first floor you have Christology, the study of Jesus, and for most of us, that is a big living room (which is not a bad thing, to be clear). Then you have other important rooms, like ecclesiology (what you believe about the church) and soteriology (what you believe about salvation). For a lot of us, we are not quite sure where to put the rooms like demonology, spiritual warfare, Satan, or hell. Maybe we feel like they should be on the first floor, but honestly, we would rather they be in the attic or basement where we can keep the door locked and never go in.

In the first section of this book, we will discuss three important topics, one in each chapter, to ensure we have a full picture of what Scripture says about them. Again, entire books (and collections of books) have been written on some of the things we are going to cover in a chapter. But I hope to paint a picture of what the Bible says and how I have seen it play out in real life. We are going to talk about hell, Satan, and demons and try to define our theology around those topics, because even Jesus-loving, Bible-believing Christians seem to struggle to articulate what they believe about them.

In the same way the CIA seeks to gather intelligence about enemies that might want to harm us, or a quarterback studies his opponent's previous games to look for their tendencies, we must study the Enemy if we ever want to have any hope of achieving victory. Understanding who our Enemy is will kick-start our journey to living the full and abundant John 10:10 life that we all deeply desire.

CHAPTER 1

WELCOME TO HELL

WHEN MY OLDEST DAUGHTER WAS FOUR YEARS OLD, she loved lollipops more than any human being has ever loved anything. If you have ever had a four-year-old of your own (or met one, for that matter) you know they can develop these strange obsessions where their little minds are consumed by one thing and one thing only. For Presley, it was lollipops. She had a superhuman ability to spot them everywhere. When she saw one from across the room wherever we were, her eyes would get big and she would fixate on it until it was in her possession. She would give her left arm for a lollipop.

One particular day, I had taken my wife's car to a shop to get it worked on, and there at the counter was a bowl of lollipops. I thought about Presley. I try to be a fun dad, and I wanted her to know I had been thinking about her, so I grabbed one for her. I thought, *Hey, I'm going to go home a hero. I will walk in the door, declare that Daddy is home, then, "Oh, look what I have."* I played it out in my mind and thought that was exactly how it was going to go.

I got in the car to drive home and called my wife, Monica, to let her know I was on the way. I could tell she was a little frustrated, a little irritated, maybe even a little exasperated. Being the intuitive husband that I am, I asked, "What's wrong?"

She said, "Oh, Presley's had a hard day today."

"What do you mean? What did she do?"

Monica then walked me through a play-by-play of how she had struggled throughout the day. Then she said, "You know, when you get home, you're going to have to discipline her."

Ugh. My grand entry as the hero of the day suddenly seemed unlikely to happen. Parenting side note: There is no parenting university you can go to where they teach you how to discipline your kids. It is like one long practice in trying to make the punishment fit the crime. It is always a challenge.

With a game plan in mind, I walked in and said, "Hey, Presley, we need to talk. Can you go to your room and wait for me there?" She trudged to her room, almost like she knew this was coming. When I walked in, I asked, "Hey, how was your day today?" She just hung her head in shame. She said, "Daddy, I didn't make good choices today." Straight to the point.

Squatting down next to her, I asked, "Well, why not? What did you do?" She started listing it out point by point, like she had memorized it all in her head. In hindsight, I think she was thinking, *Hey, maybe if I just come clean, it will be okay.* She told me everything. One after the other. "I was mean to my sister. I was disrespectful to Mommy. I did this. I did this. I did this. I did this." Monica was right—it had been a tough day.

As she rattled off her confessions, I listened to all of them. Then I reached into in my pocket and said, "Hey, I got you something today." Her eyes got big and that perfect smile stretched across her face. She was thinking, *I bet he's going to teach me about grace!* Then I dropped the hammer and said, "But I can't give it to you now, and I hate that." And I tossed it in the trash.

She looked at me, the smile morphed into a scowl, and she yelled, "Ahhhh! I can do whatever I want!" and then a full-blown fit began. I thought, *Wow, what just happened?* Again, no one teaches you about this at parenting school. And this isn't even the chapter on demon possession!

Now what am I going to do? I just stood there watching her and thinking about my next move. Here is what was going through my mind in that moment: *I have a suite of options at this point as far as discipline goes. I could go old school and spank her. I could take away privileges, like no desserts for ten years. I could go with "I want you to spend the rest of the night with your nose in the corner." So many options at my disposal.*

At that moment, the lightbulb went off in my brain. What Presley didn't know was that I had a small collection of lollipops that I had been building just for her. I had been overseas coming back from a mission trip and had stumbled across an amazing candy shop, full of flavors she didn't even know existed. There were See's Candies Lollypops, Blow Pops, and those multicolored ones that were the size of her face. This collection was the kind of thing four-year-olds dream of.

I asked her to wait right there while I went and got the box out of my closet. I brought them back into the room, grabbed a trash can, and very slowly (and dramatically) dumped the whole stash into the trash can. As her eyes welled up with tears again, she started to weep and yell about "her" lollipops. Now they were gone, and this goodness that she didn't even know existed three minutes before was something she was going to miss out on forever. Now, before you cast your judgment on me, just remember: Everything in parenting is a discipleship opportunity.

But here is one that never even crossed my mind. At no point did I ever consider going back in there and saying, "Hey, Presley. I have really enjoyed being your dad. These have been four really great years that we have had together. But all good things must end, so now we are done. So, if you will walk with me to the front door, we have an Uber waiting on you and they are going to take you away. The rest of us will stay here. Please do not visit; that will only make things more difficult. This is done."

For the record, I would never do that (and hopefully no one ever would). But here's the problem: I think a lot of us struggle with this idea of, *Is that what God does?* When you think about an eternal punishment and there being a place of judgment and separation from God called hell, it seems like we sin, He ends up disappointed in us, and He sends us on our way. It feels like He's simply sending bad people to this place of judgment, and it is a really heavy thing to process.

Right now, you might be thinking about people who died and you do not know where they are today. Or you are thinking about people who are alive and you have no idea where they stand with Jesus. It is a sobering thing to think about. Even when you share your faith, this is one of the things that prevents us from talking about Jesus. We are going in with the good news and we think in the back of their minds others are thinking, *Oh, you think I am going to hell, huh? That is the only reason you are talking to me right now.*

It feels like so much judgment, so we struggle and wrestle with the idea. If you are wrestling with it, I am glad you are, because to me it says you understand the weightiness of the matter and the urgency of the topic. We'll come back to my lollipop story later in the chapter because I think it helps us understand what actually happens in hell.

A STATE OF CONFUSION

Even as I share the gospel with people, I see a movement toward apathy on this topic. Although I have the natural wiring of an evangelist, I believe that *every* Christian is called to pass their faith on to others. I try to have multiple gospel conversations each week, and I have noticed a shift through the years. When I first became a Christian about twenty years ago and I would share the gospel with people, I would run into an attitude of, "Hey, I want no part in worshiping a God who sends somebody to hell. I want nothing to do with that God."

Now it seems I tend to run into the attitude of, "Eh, I don't know. Who cares? I know I'm alive right now. Someday I'm going to die, but hopefully not anytime soon. Who knows? Maybe the lights just go off. I'm not sure where you go. Heaven. Hell. Who can really know? I'm just not going to think about it right now."

Truthfully, it is almost too easy for the villain at this point because it seems like Christians are not even on the same page. Every two years, Ligonier Ministries and Lifeway Research partner together and create a report called the State of Theology where they poll US evangelicals and ask them about a variety of cultural hot-button issues, as well as certain theological beliefs to see what people believe. As a pastor, it is a fascinating report to read (and I encourage all Christians to read it because it is data we all need to know).

It is also (at times) disheartening to read. In the 2022 study, respondents were presented with the statement, "Hell is a real place where certain people will be punished forever." They were then asked if they strongly or somewhat agreed (or disagreed), or if they were unsure. Based on their findings, 59 percent agreed with the statement, 12 percent were not sure, and 29 percent of evangelicals in the US disagreed.[1] Because it is easy to define terms differently, here's the definition of *evangelical* they used in the study, meaning all respondents strongly agreed with all of the following statements:

- The Bible is the highest authority for what I believe.
- It is very important for me personally to encourage non-Christians to trust Jesus Christ as their Savior.

- Jesus Christ's death on the cross is the only sacrifice that could remove the penalty of my sin.
- Only those who trust in Jesus Christ alone as their Savior receive God's free gift of eternal salvation.

These were not random people who were surveyed at a mall or a theme park. These are people who hold orthodox beliefs, trust the authority of Scripture, and believe Jesus is the only way to eternal life. Even among that group, only three out of five believe that hell is a *real* place where people will spend an eternity separated from God.

WOW

AN UNPLEASANT REALITY

In a book about the spiritual realm, it's important to develop a proper understanding of the nature of heaven and hell. I will show you my cards: I believe there are two places, heaven and hell, where human souls go once we die. Again, really intelligent people have written a lot of books on hell and what it is. We do not have the time or space here for all those thoughts, but we do need a high-level framework for what hell is if we are going to understand its role in the spiritual realm.

When the Scriptures talk about hell, what are they talking about? There are a few things we know. First, it is very difficult for us to comprehend hell because we have no real framework for it here on earth. There is no such thing as hell on earth because in the worst place on earth, experiencing the worst thing you could possibly imagine you'd experience on earth, you still sit under what is called common grace. That is, a bit of God still exists in even the worst situation.

We experience the common grace of God here on earth. In

heaven, it's the fullness of the goodness of God. On earth, there are remnants of the goodness of God. In hell, there is nothing of the goodness of God. In hell, there is nothing good. Not one thing we could think of. Some people think, *Well, I am going to go to hell and party with my friends.* No, you won't. There is no beer in hell. There are no shots of tequila in hell. There is nothing to numb your pain in hell. There is no laughter. There is no smiling. There is no such thing as temporary escape. There is nothing you can think of that would bring you any joy there. That is because there is *nothing* of God there. The only thing of God in hell is His wrath and His judgment of your sin.

We need to understand an important concept: Hell is a subtraction. It is subtracting out the goodness of God. When you have light and you subtract light, you are left with darkness. When you have comfort and you subtract comfort, you are left with pain. Anything good in this world comes from God. James, the half brother of Jesus, even wrote that in the Scriptures, saying, "Every good and perfect gift is from above, coming down from the Father of the heavenly lights" (James 1:17). When you subtract the Father of heavenly lights, the goodness of God, you are left with only evil.

When Jesus talked about this place, both in Matthew 10 and Mark 9, He called it Gehenna. Gehenna was a real place south of Jerusalem. It was a dump. It was a dark, horrific place of rotting flesh. It's where those who couldn't afford a burial would be thrown out. Gehenna was where worms and maggots would feast on the flesh of the dead. Child sacrifice was common there.[2] It was the place where garbage was burned and all the waste and feces of the city would go. It's like Jesus was saying, "You know that place of stench and death and worms? This is worse than that. That is the closest I can get to describing what it is so you can picture it in your mind."

It's also important for us to understand that *hell is constant pain—forever* (2 Thessalonians 1:9). Here is why this matters: Pain is only bearable when there is hope. When you experience physical pain here on earth, you think, *I am going to be okay. There is a medication for this. I can take morphine or Advil or something to numb that. Or I am going to sleep at some point.* In the bleakest of situations, as your body is failing, you may even cling to the hope that death awaits you and the pain will end. You have a hope of remedy. In hell, there is no hope of that pain ever subsiding. That is so heavy!

Now imagine the worst pain you have ever felt. I don't know what it is for you, but I would imagine something popped into your head right away. Some of you probably thought about giving birth (with or without an epidural). You may even be mad at me right now for reminding you of the pain you felt!

I have not given birth. (Surprise, surprise.) But I have had a kidney stone (several, in fact). I am not here to tell you it is worse than giving birth because I am smarter than that and I would never do that. But I can tell you that the worst thing about the kidney stone was that the pain was constant. I had no way to know when it was going to go away. Even though I could treat it with medication, it felt like it would last forever.

Maybe it was stubbing your toe. You were walking in full stride and you jammed it on the corner of the bed. Pinkie toe. Boom! Is it broken? You were doing that dance, all while trying to stay quiet even though you wanted to say those words you could not say because God is watching. It hurt so bad, but you knew it was going to go away. But what if it didn't? What if it stayed that painful for the rest of your life? Imagine what that would be like.

In hell, that pain is not going to go away. It is forever. Not a hundred years, not a hundred billion years. Not two hundred billion years. There is no sleep, no numbing, no hope of it going away. Again, that is a heavy thing to think about.

Hell is also a place of *eternal regret and unsatisfied longing.*

What makes hell so horrific is an understanding of all you could have had in God and your choice to refuse it. You then end up with eternal regret. You may have heard of FOMO, or the fear of missing out. Hell is eternal FOMO.

Remember the story at the beginning of the chapter? Presley missed out on the goodness I had for her because of the consequences of her actions. At that point, all she could do was regret that she missed out. In Luke 16, Jesus told the story of a rich man dressed in fine clothes who died and ended up in hell. What's fascinating about the story is the posture of the rich man. He was not mad at God that he was in hell. He knew he deserved it. He was full of shame and regret, thinking about what could have been. To make it even worse, he could see heaven! He caught a glimpse of what he had truly missed out on.

When I was a child, I went to Disney World. I had never been outside of Texas and had never ridden on a roller coaster, so when the opportunity came to go to the happiest place on earth, you can imagine my excitement. We loaded up a bus with other people from our church and made the trek from Texas to Florida. Finally we arrived, and I was in line to ride my first roller coaster.

In that line, something went terribly wrong in my stomach. Have you ever had a cramp in your calf where it just closes up and you can't walk? That happened in my intestines. I literally fell over in pain. I thought that was it for me. I was there in Disney World in the fetal position in line for this roller coaster. Somebody called for help and the next thing I knew I was being loaded onto a gurney and taken to the infirmary.

There I sat in tremendous pain, but the pain was not the worst part. It was that they put me right beside a window. I could hear the laughter of all my friends, the joyful screams of them coming down the roller coasters, and I realized all I was going to miss out on because of this stupid cramp. Now, that is a trivial illustration for what awaits the eternity of those who reject God. It's painful. There is suffering. It's eternal. It's uncomfortable.

This reality is not pleasant. It should give us a feeling in the pit of our stomachs as we process what that means for the people we live next door to, work alongside, and interact with on a daily basis. It is sobering and should ignite in us a passion for sharing the good news of Jesus with everyone we meet (but more on that later).

In the nineteenth and twentieth centuries, there was a growing movement of "hellfire and brimstone" preachers whose sole message was to "turn or burn" (meaning accept Jesus or else) so you did not end up experiencing the wrath of hell. Following Jesus merely became an extra insurance policy. Then the preacher would move on to the next town with the same message. In an effort to not be "those Christians," we have become so uncomfortable with the reality of hell and eternal separation from God that instead of using it as motivation to expand the kingdom of God, we (either consciously or subconsciously) let it fade to the back of our minds.

We have adopted an "out of sight, out of mind" mentality that diminishes hell, and it ultimately bleeds into much more of our spiritual life than we realize. The rapper Eminem said, "There's a place called heaven and a place called hell. A place called prison and a place called jail, and da-da's probably on his way to all of them except one."[3] This is the nonchalant attitude we have toward a place of eternal torment. But every single person you know— every person you've ever interacted with, and every person who has ever lived—will be in either heaven or hell one day, forever.

MORE THAN A TOURIST TRAP

A couple of years ago, as summer was fast approaching, I was tasked with finding a destination for our family's big summer vacation. Monica had only two stipulations for me. The first was that I couldn't pair it with a speaking engagement. The second was that I needed to be completely "off" (no late-night responding to emails, no quick work text messages, no nothing) and fully present with them. Admittedly, that can be a challenge for me, but I knew she was right, so I agreed and the search began.

I was busy searching for travel deals when a friend reached out and generously said we could use their condo in Grand Cayman. We had never been, but I am a beach guy, so all the pictures of crystal blue water, palm trees, and sugar-white sand were alluring. It was an easy sell for me. We found the right week, booked the airfare, and planned our trip!

When the day came, travel went exceptionally smoothly, and the island did not disappoint. It was the most perfect beach I've ever seen. The water is the kind of blue a camera just can't quite capture. It felt like a little commercial for heaven. So, imagine my confusion when I saw a sign that said, "This Way to Hell." I ignored the first one, but then there was another sign, complete with colorful flames all around it. "This Way to Hell," the second one read. By this point, my curiosity got the best of me, and I pulled up Google Maps. Sure enough, in the middle of the island, not too far from where we were staying, was a place called Hell.

One morning my son, Weston, and I got up early to go to the grocery store and the signs for Hell were *everywhere*. Weston yelled, "Dad, look! That sign says H-E-double hockey sticks!" We were really close by. "Do you want to go?" I asked. He was pretty apprehensive, which I appreciated. That felt like a parenting job well done. But we were so close and I was so intrigued that we couldn't *not* go see it.

We pulled up to an old, rundown store that was painted a bright, fire-engine red (go figure). There was a cutout of a devil and a platform that looked out over a field of jagged volcanic rock. Imagine a large area of charcoal spikes protruding out of the ground. Someone apparently thought, *Hey, this must be what hell looks like.* Then they put a carved devil statue in the middle of it and made a tourist trap.

We walked into the store and a young woman wearing devil horns said, "Hi, welcome to Hell. How is your day going?" Another man, presumably the owner, also wearing horns and a pointed tail said, "How in the hell are you?" There were shirts and shot glasses and other souvenirs for sale printed with "hell" colloquialisms and cliches. It was an oddly cheery place.

This is what we've done with hell. We've made it a tourist trap. The Enemy has tricked us into thinking he's some kind of villain in a Marvel movie, or a chubby cherub selling tacos. In reality, he's the mastermind behind every rape, every murder, and every kind of evil. Including the evil *you* do. Even the evil you're blind to, because you've tricked yourself into thinking, *It's not that bad.* In doing so, you've partnered with the Prince of Darkness and invited him to be your friend, knowingly or not.

We have two choices as Christ followers. We can continue on in our day-to-day existence, oblivious to the realities of what is going on all around us, and follow Jesus as best we can until we die someday. But I believe that kind of life puts a ceiling on our ability to live that full life we talked about. The alternative (and the one I propose) is that we learn all that we can. If we familiarize ourselves with this Enemy and how he operates we can maximize our seventy-six years (give or take) here on earth.

If that is the route we choose, we must start at the beginning and understand the origin story of the one waging war against us. The villain we're talking about is the one leading the spiritual war against you.

MAKE IT STICK: PAUSE AND REFLECT

1. Hell is described as a place of eternal pain, regret, and unsatisfied longing. How does this description challenge or affirm your current understanding of hell? How does it impact your view of God's judgment and justice?

2. Some Christians have become uncomfortable with the reality of hell and have adopted an "out of sight, out of mind" mentality. Do you see this attitude reflected in your own life or in your broader Christian community? How can we maintain a balanced perspective on hell that acknowledges its reality without losing sight of God's love and grace?

3. Think back on the tourist trap in Grand Cayman called Hell. How does this story highlight the way society has trivialized hell? How can we avoid minimizing the seriousness of hell while still engaging in conversations about it?

CHAPTER 2

MISTAKEN IDENTITY

RECENTLY, I BECAME REALLY INTERESTED IN SNAKES.
Before you cast your judgment upon me, I will admit: It is a weird thing to suddenly become interested in as a fortysomething-year-old man, but here we are. My whole life I had been afraid of snakes. Not just "I don't like snakes," but legitimately afraid of them. I grew up on a farm and had always been told that the only good snake is a dead snake. Every snake, regardless of where I saw it or what it looked like, was venomous and wanted to do nothing more than hunt me down and kill me.

What changed? Well, I'm naturally a curious guy, so I joined a couple of Facebook groups full of people all around Texas who are experts at identifying snakes. Before that point, I would try to identify each snake I saw. I would see one near a body of water and say, "Oh, there is a water moccasin." As I'd walk around the neighborhood, one would slither across the street and I would declare, "Another copperhead." Once, I did this while walking with a friend of mine (who has an actual understanding of snakes) and he said, "No, that one is actually a plain-bellied water snake. Those are harmless. Stop trying to figure out how to kill it and just run away." This kept happening over and over. I would try to identify it first and he would correct me.

Anytime I saw a snake, my habit was to pinpoint it as a dangerous snake and tell Monica we should just list the house and move somewhere less treacherous. But then I discovered some Facebook groups where the sole purpose of the group was to identify the snakes people posted. And these people do not play around. These are no-nonsense groups—trust me. They want no part in your clever rhymes that misidentify the snake that you just saw in your front yard. They want a couple of pictures and your location, and they can tell you exactly what you are dealing with and how concerned you should be.

Here is what I learned after a few short weeks: I actually knew *nothing* about snakes. Let me just share some truth with you. I live in Texas, where there are over 105 species of snakes. Of those, only four kinds (yes, four) are venomous: cottonmouths, copperheads, coral snakes, and rattlesnakes. As it turns out, the vast, *vast* majority of the snakes you encounter are absolutely harmless to you. In fact, some of them are more dangerous to other snakes than people!

If you are having a conversation on your patio and there is a kingsnake in the corner, and you see it, there is not a chance that you're like, "Oh, look at that cute little snake in the corner. So, how have you been this weekend?" No, you are jumping up and grabbing the shovel, everyone is running inside, and pandemonium is ensuing. But the truth is, you are safer with that kingsnake there in the corner than you are with it cut in half because of your shovel. Why? Kingsnakes eat copperheads and venomous snakes. That's what they do. That's why they're the "king." Rat snakes eat rodents. See, they can be helpful!

Now, I know I am not, in just a few paragraphs, going to convince you to love snakes. I get it. But here's what I do want you to know: When it comes to snakes, we have been so poorly trained and equipped to identify which ones can harm us that we don't know which ones are out to legitimately harm us. Our thinking has been skewed and we are unable to call out our enemies.

We have done the same thing with Satan. We have condensed the "ruler of the kingdom of the air" (Ephesians 2:2), the one whose sole mission is to oppose God and His plans here on earth, into a chubby little red guy with horns and a pitchfork. We have been conditioned to think that way since we were kids and there were cartoons with a little devil on one shoulder and an angel on the other with an internal struggle between right and wrong playing out onscreen before our young eyes. We aren't taught who he is or what his tactics actually look like day-to-day. For some, our theology never moves much beyond that visual image.

UNAWARE AND UNAFFECTED

C. S. Lewis, in his book *The Screwtape Letters*, said this about our belief about the Enemy:

> There are two equal and opposite errors into which our race can fall about the devils. One is to disbelieve in their existence. The other is to believe, and to feel an excessive and unhealthy interest in them.[1]

C. S. Lewis was calling out the error of not believing there is an enemy. Of saying, "Ah, whatever. Who knows?" The other mistake is to make too much of him. We all have a friend like that, who believes he's in every bush and around every corner, ready to jump out and get you when you are least expecting it.

I think there is a third error. Now, I am by no means claiming to be smarter than C. S. Lewis. He wins! But in this modern-day existence, particularly among Christians, I've seen a new error crop up. Many of us believe there's an enemy; we believe there are devils, demons, and evil. If I were to say, "True or false: Satan is real," my hunch is that most of you reading this right now would answer "True." And it would have *zero* implications on how you live.

Think about what you did yesterday, from the time you woke up until the time you went to bed. How many times did you filter your decision-making through the lens of "What does the Enemy want me to do?" In making decisions, we are not thinking, *Well, what does the Enemy want? What is he after? How is he at work? What is he capable of?* We don't even understand that. Instead, we are unaware and unaffected, which is exactly where I believe the Enemy wants us. Because this battle is happening in an unseen realm, it is easy for us to forget (or worse, not care) that it is taking place all around us. It leaves us unable to identify the villain trying to kill us, all while that very same villain is moving the goalposts and creating a world of chaos and confusion for everyone, but in particular for followers of Jesus.

The truth is, the Bible gives us more of an origin story for Satan than most believers realize. In fact, all throughout the Bible there are biographical tidbits that, when pieced together, give us a fuller picture of who exactly we are fighting. Our problem is that we likely have not taken the time to put all those pieces together. A great starting point comes from a chapter that likely is not printed on a single coffee mug in your collection: Ezekiel 28.

THE KING OF TYRE AND A FALLEN ANGEL

Most believers already know the narrative: Satan was an angel in heaven. Early on he became prideful and decided to stand up in opposition to God. God kicked him out of heaven, sent him to earth, and then one day he appeared in the garden of Eden in the form of a serpent. That narrative comes from Ezekiel 28, but it is not explicitly clear from a surface-level reading of the text.

Ezekiel is an apocalyptic prophetic text, which a lot of Christians put under the category of "books that are too confusing to understand," but the Holy Spirit kept these passages in the Bible for a reason! In the Old Testament, prophets were chosen by God to discern situations to tell the people God's will. In the midst of something happening, they would say, "Hey, this is what God is doing. Let me explain it to you." Ezekiel was no exception, but his style was different. We see in his book that Ezekiel would take current events and speak, through those current events, timeless truths. He explained these theological truths through the lens of what was happening all around them in the time and space they occupied. He was a master at contextualizing his message.

At the beginning of this important passage in Ezekiel 28, Ezekiel was talking about the king of Tyre, who was a real king. On top of that, Tyre was a real place, just north of Israel (today it is in Lebanon). Ezekiel started by talking to a king who had amassed great wealth, won battles, and become very powerful. Ezekiel started calling him out with a word from the Lord, but then in the middle of calling him out and talking about current events, he pivoted and started to talk about Satan.

It would be like if I said, "Vladimir Putin invaded Ukraine, and I remember when he fell from heaven and a third of the angelic realm fell with him." *I'm sorry, what?* It would feel like a conversational whiplash. We were just talking about the news, then the conversation went somewhere weird. With a 2D reading of Scripture, this all seems disconnected. But when we dig deeper, we get a 4K understanding of what is going on as Satan is described. Here is what Ezekiel 28:11–14 says:

The word of the LORD came to me: "Son of man, take up a lament concerning the king of Tyre and say to him: 'This is what the Sovereign LORD says:

> "'You were the seal of perfection,
>   full of wisdom and perfect in beauty.
> You were in Eden,
>   the garden of God;
> every precious stone adorned you:
>   carnelian, chrysolite and emerald,
>   topaz, onyx and jasper,
>   lapis lazuli, turquoise and beryl.
> Your settings and mountings were made of gold;
>   on the day you were created they were prepared.
> You were anointed as a guardian cherub,
>   for so I ordained you.
> You were on the holy mount of God;
>   you walked among the fiery stones.'"

Follow me here: This is Satan's origin story. There is a shift away from talking about the king of Tyre and toward talking about Satan instead. It tells us that he was a beautiful angel and he was even in Eden, the place where all was right and perfect in the world before sin entered the picture. That should be problematic for us, right? I was always taught that Eden was perfect before man sinned. How did the villain get there?

And that list of stones in Ezekiel is not just a list of rocks you would find in a creek bed. Those were the nine stones from the priestly garments referenced in Exodus 28. God was nodding His head at the reality that He had some sort of special service for Satan. This magnificent angel was different from the others. Many scholars believe the phrase "settings and mountains" is a reference to musical instruments. So, Satan is described here as a beautiful angel with a priestly designation who played musical instruments. It is as if God were describing Satan as the OG worship leader. *Wait, what?!*[2]

Then we read about Satan being anointed as a guardian cherub. Here is where Hallmark has done us a disservice. When you hear cherub, you think of a greeting card, right? You think of a chubby little angel with cute little wings and rosy cheeks. You think of Cupid, if you will (which is stupid, if you will). It is incorrect thinking because anytime guardian cherubs reveal themselves to creation in Scripture, the next two words you usually see are "Get up" or "Fear not." Why? Because they are insanely huge, powerful creatures.

A PROUD HEART

Now, see what Ezekiel says about Satan's rebellion:

> "'You were blameless in your ways
>> from the day you were created
>> till wickedness was found in you.
> Through your widespread trade
>> you were filled with violence,
>> and you sinned.
> So I drove you in disgrace from the mount of God,
>> and I expelled you, guardian cherub,
>> from among the fiery stones.
> Your heart became proud
>> on account of your beauty,
> and you corrupted your wisdom
>> because of your splendor.

So I threw you to the earth;
   I made a spectacle of you before kings.
By your many sins and dishonest trade
   you have desecrated your sanctuaries.
So I made a fire come out from you,
   and it consumed you,
and I reduced you to ashes on the ground
   in the sight of all who were watching.
All the nations who knew you
   are appalled at you;
you have come to a horrible end
   and will be no more.'" (28:15–19)

This helps paint a more complete picture for us of what actually happened to Satan. At some point in history, God made Satan along with the entire angelic realm. He made the heavenly hosts, the angel armies. All these beings were created to reflect the glory of God and to carry out His will, both in heaven and on earth. But that role was not enough for one angel named Satan. He was a beautiful, worship-leading angel—blameless, even! But that was not enough for him. Scripture tells us he wanted *more*. His heart became too proud, and his heart became corrupt, so God drove him, in disgrace, out of His presence.

God made him special, but he became evil. This presents us with a theological conundrum: Did God create evil? Is evil God's doing? The answer is no. The text says very plainly that God created Satan good. God is saying, "I made you perfect in beauty. And then you rebelled." But God did create the *possibility* of evil.

You see, the only way that something can be good is if it *could be* bad. If it could not be bad, it would not be good. It would just . . . be. Think about it this way: Light is a thing. Darkness, on the other hand, is *no thing*. Darkness is simply the *absence* of light.

If you insert light, you have light. If you pull the light aw
you're left with in the void and emptiness is darkness.
way to think about it is with heat. If you withdraw heat, you are
left with cold. Cold only exists because heat exists. Without heat,
cold would not be cold; it just would be.

God is good, and goodness marks Him. If you pull back good,
what you are left with in the void is evil. Godliness is a thing, so
ungodliness is what you are left with when you withdraw godliness from the equation. We could play this game with a thousand
different variables, but I think you get my point: Evil is the absence
of good.

KICKED OUT OF HEAVEN

When I was in high school, I was briefly kicked out of school.
Here's what happened: I had a master plan to skip school. My
brother had a big brick of a cell phone like Zack Morris from *Saved
by the Bell*, back before anyone else had cell phones. I had a friend
with pretty handwriting write a note saying that I had been feeling sick, so if I went downhill at school to go ahead and call "my
dad" (which was actually my brother's cell phone), and send me
home. She signed it as if she were my mom. I was going to then
have the whole day to hang out with my friends and my girlfriend,
who lived in the next town over and did not have school that day.
Brilliant plan, right?

It turned into a bad execution of *Ferris Bueller's Day Off*. I
faked a cough, turned in my note, and my friends picked me up
outside. The attendance clerk, who did not play her part right
at all, compared the handwriting on the note to past notes and
noticed it was different. Then she noticed "my dad's" phone number had changed. She then called my mom to ask her if she had

sent me to school with a note, and my mom had no idea what she was talking about. Who knew this attendance clerk was basically Sherlock Holmes?

My mom called my dad (and my friend and coconspirator's dad) and they decided we would talk about it at the end of the day. When we were driving home and stopped at a stoplight, I looked over at the truck next to us and I knew we were done for. Five feet from me was my dad, this stoic, John Wayne–esque man, staring at me through his open window and just shaking his head.

Once we got home, we were grounded by our parents and suspended from school on top of that. I got in trouble because I didn't go to school, and now they were telling me I couldn't go to school? They decided we were such menaces to society that they would rather not even have us in the building. They knew we were the troublemakers, so they decided they would rather us cause trouble on the outside than the inside. We got kicked out.

We often hear that Satan fell from heaven. If you are anything like me, that gives you a mental image of someone tripping and falling, like if someone fell off a building or into the Grand Canyon. Like he stepped on the wrong cloud. But Satan didn't trip and tumble out. This passage in Ezekiel makes it really clear that God kicked him out; He expelled Satan from heaven.

Scripture goes out of its way to describe just how blessed Satan had been. But because of his rebellion and his pride, he was sent to earth, and now there is this cosmic test going on every single moment of every single day. Read this carefully: You and I are in the test. Who are you going to worship? God, the Creator of the heavens and the earth, or the prince of this era? Paul referred to Satan as the "god of this age" in 2 Corinthians 4:4, meaning Satan is actively involved in the here and now of daily life. So, which way will you go? Every day we have to choose.

Here is the most mind-bending part of all this: You can sit

in church on a Sunday morning and worship Satan. We think of satanism as something way different, but the truth is, he does not need you to worship him with Ouija boards, seances, lit candles, and sacrifices.

When you worship *anything other than God*, Satan will accept that as worship to himself. In fact, he would probably prefer that you do not even waste your time with the Ouija boards and candles, because that's weird, and then you would not have friends, and therefore you would have no influence. What he really wants you to do is worship anything other than God and influence as many others as possibly to do the same. This is his tactic, and he carries it out every day here on earth.

To be abundantly clear: Satan is not in hell. It's a theological misunderstanding and a categorical mistake to say that he is. Hell is a place created for Satan to ultimately serve his eternal judgment (Revelation 20:10). We operate with a misunderstanding that Satan functions as the CEO of hell, but where do we see that in the Scriptures? We love to create distance between us and him, but biblically that's innacurate. We love to think, *We're up here and he's down there, so the distance keeps us safe,* but that's not actually true. Eventually, at the end of all days, he will be cast there after the last battle. But right now, Satan is roaming around the earth like a roaring lion looking for someone to devour, according to 1 Peter 5:8.

To add another layer to this, it is important to know that he is not everywhere. Satan is not omnipresent. So, it is also a categorical mistake to say, "Satan did this to me." Most likely (although it's impossible to say for certain), Satan himself has never been anywhere near you. He has likely never even been in the same zip code as you, unless he was just visiting for some influential event. Wherever there is an abnormal amount of death, destruction, disease, genocide, or other kinds of wickedness—that's likely where Satan is. Wherever there are people of great influence—he's probably there. Revelation 12 tells us that a third of the angelic realm came with him, so he is not alone, and they are down here with us too (but we will get to them in the next chapter). Satan has help, so he doesn't have to be everywhere to make his mark.

WHY DOES IT HAVE TO BE THIS WAY?

For a long time in my life, even as a believer, I wrestled with the *why* in this entire discussion. Why did this have to be the narrative? Why not just skip all the chaos, death, and destruction and keep things perfect like they were in the garden of Eden? Am I the only one who thinks that is a better solution?

Here's where I've landed. As Christians, we do not believe in dualism, which implies that God and Satan are equal forces going at it in the ring and we are out in the crowd wondering who will be declared the winner. No, God created Satan, and He has dominion and authority over him. This is not even like David and Goliath. This is Goliath versus a cream puff. Satan must ask God for permission to do stuff (see the story of Job). But why does God allow it?

What if when Satan said, "Hey, I don't want to worship You. I want to be like You," God had responded with a snap of His fingers and said, "Oh, you want to be like Me? Be no more"? And then poof, he was gone. And we all just carried on with our lives from there. My hunch is that if He would have done that, there would have been no way for you and me to know that God is good. If time and time again God just obliterates anything that comes against Him, how would we know that He is actually any good at all?

Based on a common interpretation of Revelation 12, the Bible indicates a third of the angelic realm went with Satan. So when this all happened, a third of the angels must have been questioning and wondering if He is a good God after all. And God, in an incredible act of mercy, said, "Great—we'll see what happens." And He sent Satan here to earth with an army of fallen angels. God then created us out of the manifestation of love between the Father, Son, and Holy Spirit, made in His image, and said, "Okay, Satan, you can try to rule over them if you want. But I am going to show them something better at every turn. And they will choose who they desire to serve. Me or any other god, which is you."

That is the narrative you and I live in every single day. Think about all the opportunities you have throughout any given day to serve the God who created the universe or the villain who seeks to steal an abundant life from you. It all traces back to what God was describing in Ezekiel 28. That is the story we are a part of, your parents were part of, and your great-great-great-great-great-great-grandparents were part of too. We feel it and sense it is happening all around us. We have even seen this play out in movies a hundred times. It's the plot of most movies from the time we were children. Someone is going to a foreign land to fight a battle to see if good or evil is ultimately the winner.

This is the script that Disney and Marvel and DC and others have made billions of dollars from. They are just swapping out the variables. In those meeting rooms they are saying, "Do we want her to be a kind of princess who talks to animals? What about two sisters, but one of them can turn things into ice? Or do we want her to be a stepsister with a stepmother? Or a fairy godmother? Or maybe up in a tower with long hair? And then we can send in the prince to rescue her? Scrap that, we should make this one about lions. Maybe it's two lions. We will call them Mufasa and Scar, and we will figure out who is going to be the king of the jungle."

Over and over and over, whether it's the Avengers, the Justice League, Snow White, or Harry Potter, you've seen this. And you wonder: Why does it resonate so deeply within your heart? It's because this is the story you live in. That's why you're seeing it over and over and over again. It doesn't take a lot of creativity to write these scripts; you just take the characters, change their names, tweak the plotline, alter the setting, and there you go.

But in real life, this is a far bigger battle than simply God versus Satan, good versus evil. God has an army, but Satan does too. And Satan's army is desperate to take you out.

MAKE IT STICK: OLD AND NEW

On a piece of paper, make two columns: one side with Old Beliefs and the other side with New Beliefs.

1. First, take a few minutes to jot down the beliefs you held about Satan before reading this chapter. Write down everything you knew before you started reading it.
2. Now reflect on how your understanding of Satan has evolved or changed since beginning this journey. What new insights or perspectives have you gained so far?
3. Now, in a paragraph or two, rewrite your beliefs about Satan, incorporating any new insights or changes in perspective you've experienced. Why does a fuller understanding of Satan help you in this spiritual battle?

CHAPTER 3

AN INVISIBLE ARMY

AN INTERESTING THING HAPPENS WHEN YOU start working on a book about spiritual warfare. People start telling you their own stories. I think most people are afraid of sounding "weird" or "out there," so we tend to keep these stories to ourselves. I believe that's exactly what the Enemy wants from us. But once people figured out I was a safe person to tell their stories to, they started coming. People would say things like, "Did I tell you about that time I saw a demon when I was eight years old?" Every time it would catch me by surprise. In my head, I was thinking, *We have been friends for five years and you are just now telling me you saw a demon with your own eyes?* True, that's the kind of thing I may not lead with when I first meet someone, but it would probably come out sooner than that!

Way more people have a story of their own encounter with some kind of demon than you would ever realize, which I believe is further proof that so many of us are unaware of the extent of the war going on all around us. Sometimes it's hard for them to put words to what they experienced. They will use words like *darkness* or *spirits* or *demonic,* and in a sense those words all refer to the same thing. There is so much mystery surrounding Satan's army that even finding the words to tell our stories feels like an uphill battle.

I always want to be open-minded and willing to hear these stories. I have been on mission trips all over the world, and it seems like every time, a group would come back after a day of ministry with a crazy story about a demon that was cast out. We would all celebrate—but that was never my story. Then I had an experience of my own that I will never forget. A couple of summers ago, I was in Utah for an all-guys golfing trip. A lot of the guys on the trip I already knew well. We had served in ministry together, we knew each other, and I felt a sense of "sameness" and unity on the trip. But one guy stood out. He was the guest of one of the other guys. He was about my age, would drink a little too much, drop the occasional F-bomb, and just seemed a little out of place, honestly.

On the last day we struck up a conversation and he told me his story. At first, he didn't want to, because he kept saying things like "It will sound crazy" and "You wouldn't understand." Finally, I got him to open up and he told me in detail about an experience he had one day while shopping. To sum it up, he said that when he opened his mouth, "violent and painful" voices came out. When I said, "That sounds demonic," he quickly shut me down and dismissed it. He told me that I sounded like his mom (which did not feel like a compliment). I had a sense that God was trying to draw this guy near to Himself, but the Enemy was pulling him in the opposite direction.

It was just the two of us left in the country club dining room before we were all about to head home. I asked if I could pray for him before we left. Right as I was about to start, my friend Adam, who is a passionate follower of Jesus, walked in, and I asked if he wanted to join us as we prayed together.

I began to pray, but I wasn't prepared for how that was going to go. As we prayed over this man, he began coughing, and kind of growling in between coughs. With my hand on his back, I could feel him convulsing. I cracked open my eyes to see what was going on. His hand contorted as though all the muscles in it had contracted, but he couldn't make a fist. His wrist was turned back as far as it would go. Then his arm flew out to his side, then up as though he were raising his hand for a question in the most awkward way imaginable. Then it went behind his back as though an invisible person was trying to arrest him.

His body was doubled over as the sounds he was making got louder and louder. It was like he was trying to cough something up. Or, like something (or someone?) was coming out. *Was this really happening? In a country club?!* If I'm honest, I was terrified. Out loud I was praying, "Jesus, please bind whatever demonic presence is here and please bring it out of him," but in my head I was praying, *And please don't let this thing jump on me!* I was praying two prayers at once! I didn't know what to do in this situation. I had never been taught.

In the theological circles I had been in, I was taught that this kind of thing was typically fabricated by a willing actor. That was not aligning with my present reality. Where were all my charismatic/Pentecostal friends when I needed one?! The sounds and convulsing seemed to crescendo, becoming more violent, but as I continued to pray, they calmed down after a couple of minutes. He eventually stood still and I said, "Amen."

"Well, that was unexpected," he said calmly with a surprised look on his face. He seemed embarrassed, and I was convinced that he was not the force behind what had just happened. It had been done to him. It was otherworldly. I had been writing this book on spiritual warfare, and I was beginning to question much of what I believed about it.

We parted ways with the guy and agreed to touch base later.

Adam and I were sharing a cabin, and we needed to check out, so we jumped on a golf cart to head back. I was shaking as we tried to process what had just happened. We quickly packed up, jumped in the car, and headed toward the airport. Then I found out in a group text that we were all going to stop for a quick lunch. I had the thought, *I need to share the gospel with him!*

We pulled into a Mexican restaurant, and there he was, sitting at the end of the table. "How are you feeling?" I asked him.

"I have a peace I've never had before."

"Let me ask you a couple of questions. Between one and ten, ten being certain, if you died tonight, how certain are you that you'd go to heaven?"

He said, "I would have told you a ten. But I wasn't a ten. I think I'm a ten now."

I continued, "And if you stood before God and He asked, 'Why should I let you in?' what would you say?"

"Only Jesus. That's all I could say. Jesus is the only reason I'm getting in."

Something shifted in my heart after that experience. Suddenly this took a total turn from a theoretical discussion I would have with my small group around a campfire about our beliefs on spiritual warfare. This was a boots-on-the-ground experience I had just been a part of. As I flew back to Texas, I couldn't stop thinking about what had just happened.

AN ARMY WITH AN AGENDA

As we talked about in the previous chapter, Satan is one of many demons. Too often we think about spiritual warfare as some kind of boxing match with God in one corner and Satan in the other. We know God is going to ultimately win, but we are just going to let those two fight it out. The truth is, the boxing-match image falls short; *war* really is a more accurate picture of what is going on.

As we discussed, about a third of the angelic realm came with Satan when he was kicked out of heaven. So Satan and his army are down here on earth seeking to kill, steal, and destroy (John 10:10). He is telling them where to go and what to do. They are around us, studying us, firing at us, and constantly trying to defeat us.

To understand Satan and his army of demons, we have to grab different puzzle pieces from the Scriptures and put them together to get the full picture. In the Old Testament, "demons" or "evil spirits" are mentioned in some form less than a dozen times. In the New Testament, on the other hand, that number jumps to over eighty![1] Throughout His ministry on earth, Jesus came across these spirits through the people He encountered time and time again. Let's try to understand some of the most critical pieces as we wrap our minds around this concept.

First, Satan and his army of demons have an agenda and will stop at nothing to accomplish it. We will get to *how* the Enemy does that in the next section, but for now it is important that you know they have desires for how you will live your life.

Think about all the decisions you process throughout a given day or week. Should you buy that car? They have a desire. Should you move? They have a desire. Should you let your kids do select sports? They have a desire. Satan has a will, and he uses his forces (demons) to carry it out. Should you date that person? Should you go to that concert? Should you book that vacation?

In all of life's decisions, they have a desire for you. There is something that they want to carry out in your life through those decisions. I know this sounds simplistic, but their agenda is to keep you away from the will and the goodness of God. And I believe that they major in the minor decisions of our lives with the hope that we don't realize how far off track we are getting with each seemingly inconsequential move.

A second thing to know is that they are not omnipotent (all-powerful), nor are they all-knowing. They cannot read your mind. But they *are* studying you (and have been studying people like you) so that they will know what will take you out (Luke 22:31–32). Hebrews 13:2 says that people have entertained angels without knowing it (or showed hospitality, depending on your translation). We know that demons are fallen angels and eternal beings. It makes sense that they are studying generation after generation to learn all that they can.

This is where generational sin—the idea that certain sinful patterns and behaviors are passed down from generation to generation—comes into play. As I talk to my Gen Z friends, I see a lot of confusion around generational sin, generational curses, and hereditary spirits. I hear questions like, "Are there demons assigned to my family that my great-great-great-grandparents had that are basically demons of alcoholism that we can't shake?"

I do not believe Satan commissions demons like, "Hey, you're the alcoholic demon. Go turn Tanner into an alcoholic." It is possible that alcoholism is a demon's tool of choice, and I *do* believe they study generations of people and understand the pitfalls that you are most prone to step in, based on nurture and nature. All they want to do is keep you out of right relationship with God, so they feed you and tempt you and lie to you to make you trip up in the same way that they did your great-great-great-great-grandparent. It messes with your mind, discourages you, and you believe the lie that you can never be free from it.

There is a third truth for us to understand: I believe that every human being is influenced by a spirit: either demonic spirits or the Holy Spirit. The world is first spiritual, and every human interaction in the world has spiritual implications. There is an army of evil beings trying to keep every human away from God. If we're not being influenced by the Holy Spirit, we are certainly being influenced by evil spirits. Scripture never explicitly says that Christians (who all have the Holy Spirit dwelling inside of them) cannot be possessed by demons or evil spirits, but I understand why many jump to that conclusion. In my humble opinion, we make up different labels like *possession* and *oppression* to describe what the Enemy can do. Whenever demonic possession occurs in the New Testament, it is happening in an unbeliever. However, Christians can be *influenced* by demonic spirits, which is why we are instructed to resist the devil and his forces (1 Peter 5:8–9; James 4:7).

Finally, I believe that behind *everything* broken in the world, the villain and his army are at work. I mean every heartbreak, burnout, panic attack, anxiety, death, diagnosis, hardship, and addiction . . . you name it. I am so bold as to say *everything* broken in this world is because of the Enemy, and much of the despair we experience on our journey here is from his demonic army.

You, as a Christian, need to realize that they are playing from a position of defeat. They want to watch the world burn. And you also need to know that you have everything you need to find victory over them.

JESUS' POWER OVER EVERYTHING

Of all the encounters Jesus had with demons or people possessed by them, one stands out because of the details we are given. It is a remarkable story of a showdown between Jesus and a man under the influence of many demonic spirits (we don't know the exact number, but scholars guess in the thousands based on Mark's account). Jesus was with His disciples and basically said, "Hey, we need to go across the lake to get this guy." To paint the picture of how it was going for the man, he was naked, chained up (even though he had been breaking chains), was cutting himself with rocks and shards of glass, and was screaming out. People were terrified.

This story shows up in Matthew, Mark, and Luke.[2] We have a lot of context to paint the picture of what this showdown actually looked like as Jesus came face-to-face with a human under the influence of approximately two thousand demonic forces. Luke went to great lengths to show us that Jesus was reversing the work of the villain. Here is what Luke 8 says:

> They sailed to the region of the Gerasenes, which is across the lake from Galilee. When Jesus stepped ashore, he was met by a demon-possessed man from the town. For a long time this man had not worn clothes or lived in a house, but had lived in the tombs. When he saw Jesus, he cried out and fell at his feet, shouting at the top of his voice, "What do you want with me, Jesus, Son of the Most High God? I beg you, don't torture me!" For Jesus had commanded the impure spirit to come out of the man. Many times it had seized him, and though he was chained hand and foot and kept under guard, he had broken his chains and had been driven by the demon into solitary places.
>
> Jesus asked him, "What is your name?"
>
> "Legion," he replied, because many demons had gone into him. And they begged Jesus repeatedly not to order them to go into the Abyss. (vv. 26–31)

So much happens in this story. Jesus knew there was a man possessed by thousands of demons, and pretty much said, "I have to go see this one. I have work to do. Boys, let's load up. Get in the boat. We have a mission." I believe Jesus woke up thinking about this guy, so He went to rescue him. Then this storm popped up, so fierce that it had vocational fishermen afraid for their lives. Some scholars (and I agree with them) believe this was a satanic effort to keep Jesus from saving this possessed man. Satan was being a little too opportunistic here, trying to take Jesus out before He could even get to the man. But Jesus calmed the storm, because even the weather is no match for His power.

He arrived to find the guy *enslaved* to demons. The man even said his name was Legion, which is a Roman term for thousands of soldiers. This is a military term, another reminder that we're in a battle. The demons begged Jesus not to cast them out; they wanted to keep this guy enslaved and stay right where they were. Mark's account of this story says that they begged Jesus not to send them out of the area, which is interesting. "Please don't send us out of the area!"

I have already told you that I believe areas have strongholds. I felt that when I moved our family to the great city of Waco. If there are specific demonic strongholds in different territories, this should cause us to ask the question, What is the stronghold where I live? Maybe it is cultural Christianity or materialism or drug use or voodoo, but I would guess *something* has a grip on the area where you live. But this Bible account makes it clear that these demons love to put a stake in the ground and claim their territory.

The Enemy also loves to keep people enslaved. A slave can only do what their master allows, and the Enemy and his forces want to keep you their slave. They want you to do what they receive as worship. They have one objective: to make you a slave to anything other than Christ, such as sin, addiction, and anything else the world has to offer you. This guy in Scripture is an extreme example, but this is how the power of the Enemy works in your life, for both believers and nonbelievers. When you feed something, it grows. When you feed pride, it grows. When you feed anger, it grows. When you feed jealousy, it grows. It gets bigger, and bigger, and bigger.

— JESUS SETS HIM FREE

This story has a fascinating conclusion. Let's keep reading:

> A large herd of pigs was feeding there on the hillside. The demons begged Jesus to let them go into the pigs, and he gave them permission. When the demons came out of the man, they went into the pigs, and the herd rushed down the steep bank into the lake and was drowned.
>
> When those tending the pigs saw what had happened, they ran off and reported this in the town and countryside, and the people went out to see what had happened. When they came to Jesus, they found the man from whom the demons had gone out, sitting at Jesus' feet, dressed and in his right mind; and they were afraid. Those who had seen it told the people how the demon-possessed man had been cured. Then all the people of the region of the Gerasenes asked Jesus to leave them, because they were overcome with fear. So he got into the boat and left. (Luke 8:32–37)

We can all agree that this story escalated quickly. I have been to the spot where they believe this happened. Anybody else ever picture these pigs jumping off a cliff? That is what I always pictured: a couple thousand pigs doing a swine dive off a cliff. But it is actually a steep hill. So, these pigs (Mark 5:13 tells us it was about two thousand in number, lining up with what "Legion" previously said) just went running down a hill toward the water and kept running until they all drowned.

And why the pigs? Have you ever wondered that? What a weird twist in the story. Why did they want to go in the pigs? Why do Matthew, Mark, and Luke all tell us that the demons went into the pigs? I heard Tim Keller say in a sermon on this passage that he read twenty commentaries trying to answer this question. He came to the conclusion that the Bible says the demons went into the pigs because . . . that's what happened. That's what they observed.[3] No creative writer is sitting in their English class saying, "What do we do next? I have an idea: have them go into the pigs! That will really get them! That would be a really good story." The Bible writers were there, they were observing what happened, and so they wrote down what they saw.

Here is what is interesting to me about this passage: Jesus *effortlessly* overpowered these demons. There was no showdown or struggle. Just some begging, and Jesus effortlessly setting this man free. This is what Jesus does. He set someone free who was so much more enslaved than you have ever been or ever seen. So when I hear people say, "Jesus can't help me," I think about how limiting that is to the One we believe conquered sin and death! How could we possibly think Jesus can't help us, after all we know He has done?

You think Jesus can't help your prodigal child or heal your marriage or free you from your addiction? We can be so self-absorbed that we think, *Nope. I'm hopeless for God. I know He brings the dead to life. I know at will, He can set a man free of thousands of demons, but I just really think my situation is going to throw Him for a loop. It's something He's never seen before. It's bigger than Him.*

Every single time someone comes to faith in Jesus, it's a miracle. It doesn't matter if you are a six-year-old at VBS or a drug-addicted adult or a ninety-year-old on your deathbed. Every time Jesus sets someone free, a miracle is happening. He is reversing the

Enemy's curse that goes all the way back to the fall of humanity in Genesis 3. He is setting the world back as it should be. Every. Single. Time.

UNDER THE AUTHORITY OF JESUS

One thing sticks out to me as I read through the accounts in the Gospels of Jesus interacting with the demonic forces of the world: Jesus has ultimate authority over them. We see it in this story—the demons begged Jesus because they knew, at the end of the day, that His authority always wins. In Matthew 10:1, we see Jesus give the apostles authority. Then in Matthew 28, in the Great Commission, Jesus reminds everyone that all authority is His, and that He is with us always (vv. 16–20). Let that sink in.

The more I've thought about this, the more I've dwelled on the fact that whoever has ultimate authority wins. If my wife and I are going to go on a date and I tell my son that his older sister is in charge, there has been a shift in the dynamics of our home. All of a sudden, Weston has to listen to Finley in a way that he did not before. Why? Because now Finley is an extension of us. She has authority. She is speaking on behalf of us. This principle carries over in a spiritual sense too. Jesus has ultimate authority and, if we have trusted in Christ's death and resurrection for the forgiveness of our sins, we have Jesus. Anything we ask, we are asking in His name. And demons are terrified of Jesus.

As I think back on my interaction with that man on our guys' trip, I am reminded of the fact that I didn't actually do anything. I believe I was faithful in the moment to pursue a conversation and to pray over him. But after we prayed and he felt embarrassed, my friend Adam said, "Man, don't feel embarrassed! That should just be a Wednesday for Christians. Don't sweat it." The challenge for us is to be faithful with each interaction we have and leave the rest up to Jesus.

While working on this book, I had a chance to sit down with an exorcist backstage at an event where we were both speaking. All of this subject matter was fresh in my mind, so I asked him, "How afraid should we be?"

"Not afraid at all," he responded. "Greater is He who is in you than he who is in the world" (a quote from 1 John 4:4). I'll share more about that conversation later. But for now, remember: We don't have to be afraid if we are under the authority of the all-powerful Jesus Christ.

MAKE IT STICK: DISSECTING THE DEMONIC

1. Can you think of a time you, or someone you know, encountered a demonic force or spirit of some kind? What was that experience like?

2. This chapter outlines four important realities for Christians to understand about how Satan and his demonic forces operate. Which of those stuck out to you the most, and why?

3. Why is it important for believers to remember that everything and everyone on earth is under the authority of Jesus?

PART 2

WHAT THE VILLAIN DOES

HOW WOULD THE ENEMY TAKE YOU OUT? **THINK** back to your answer from the beginning of the book. Write it down somewhere—maybe even in the margins of this book. I can assure you of this: He knows how he would do it.

A friend of mine is a really successful basketball coach. Year in and year out, his team is highly ranked. They consistently win, changing styles and philosophies based on the players on the roster. My friend is highly regarded among his peers, and his teams are always referred to as "well coached."

As he and I have talked, I've noticed how much time and preparation outside of the actual games goes into being successful. He and his staff break down hours of film of their opponents, looking for anything that will give them even the slightest edge in the next game. Then they self-scout, watching their own film and trying to uncover their tendencies in hopes of adding in layers of unpredictability. They want to catch their opponents off guard. It is a never-ending, year-round process. By understanding their opponents' tendencies, and their own, they can anticipate what is coming.

When we zoom out and look at what the Enemy does to try to pull us toward him and away from Jesus, we can do the same. We must diligently study the patterns and tendencies of the Enemy, as well as knowing where we are prone to stumble and fall into temptation. We need to analyze his most common patterns and tactics to learn how we can be successful in this spiritual battle.

If we do not understand the tactics of Satan and his army of demons, we will be crushed by them. Because here is what you need to know: They know your tendencies. They are studying you. They know your Amazon habits. They know your hashtag-clicking habits and your search history. They know your insecurities. They know when you stare at yourself in the mirror and are not happy with what you see. They have seen everything you do. They have studied you with a front-row seat. They see your children. They see everything. And they cannot do anything to you except try to get you to sin. When you sin, it's like you have fed the lion prowling around and looking for someone to devour, as 1 Peter 5:8 would say. That's what Scripture teaches us of our enemies, but for some reason we either don't often think about it or we just don't take it seriously.

The whole purpose of this section of the book is to identify the most common tactics the Enemy is using against God's people today.

As I shared earlier, I have had a front-row seat to thousands of lives over the past couple of decades in vocational ministry. I have stood up front after sermons and talked to people choking back tears, telling me the stories of all the ways the villain is ruining their lives. I have sat in living rooms with small groups in conflict, and in counseling sessions with couples who are on the brink of divorce. Every single one of their stories has a villain trying to tear their lives apart.

In this section, I want to share with you what I am seeing as a pastor. This list is not exhaustive, because the Enemy is crafty and is always scheming up new ways to take out followers of Jesus.

My vantage point is unique because I pastor a local church, but I also field a couple thousand questions each Friday on Instagram from people all over the country and the world. I've found that whether someone lives in Waco or Wisconsin or Washington, DC, the Enemy is trying to disrupt the lives of everyone in similar ways. Surveying the landscape of our world currently, I've noticed six primary ways the Enemy is attacking people:

- Destruction
- Distraction
- Deception
- Disunity
- Desensitization
- Deconstruction

When I started thinking of this list, I didn't intend to make them all start with the same letter (although I am a preacher who loves alliteration). But it's nice that it turned out that way, right? When the patterns of the Enemy all started to come together, these six stood out the most to me. If you are anything like me, you will experience all six at some point in your life. Maybe it will be all at once, maybe it will be in seasons, but at some point along the way, the Enemy will use each one of these approaches. When I've sensed each of these different kinds of attacks in my life, each season was a test of my faith.

I have experienced loss and hardship. My mind can be all over the place, torn between what I know to be true and the lies of this world. I have seen conflict fracture important relationships, even and especially inside the walls of the church. I have grown numb to the sins the Enemy makes so appealing. I have wrestled through doubts and questions and had to rebuild what I believe. As much as I wish I could say these were all one-and-done moments that are now in the past and I will never have to deal with them again, I know that may not necessarily be true. But when the Enemy attacks again, I will be more prepared than I was the first time.

Recently I read about a biosphere where a group of scientists had created a perfect environment to grow certain plants and trees. One thing they found was that the trees in this environment—complete with the perfect soil, amount of sunlight, and watering—grew up at a rapid pace. But then they fell over. They set out to discover why that happened, and I thought their conclusion was fascinating. Why did they topple over? There was no wind in the biosphere and so the trees were never tested. Their root system was not strengthened in the soil. There were no deep roots, so at the slightest hint of adversity they collapsed.[1]

So many of us have grown up in an environment where it was totally normal to carry a Bible, walk into a room, sing songs, walk out, go get Mexican food afterward, and talk about whether or not we liked the sermon or the worship setlist. Then when the Enemy comes after you, you wonder why you fall over like a tree with no roots. I have seen this in my own life and in the lives of people I love and care about.

Now, we can't control when and where we grow up in the faith. That part is not up to us. But we do need to make sure we know what's coming our way. We need to recognize tendencies and patterns—to let the roots of our faith dig in deep so when our faith is tested and the Enemy is after us, we can come out stronger on the other side.

CHAPTER 4

THE VILLAIN DESTROYS

WHILE RESEARCHING AND READING ABOUT SPIRI-tual warfare in the process of writing this book, I became more aware of everything going on around me. (That might be happening to you now while you are reading this book.) During a particular week of research, I had one of those stretches where I felt like everything was just . . . off. My spiritual warfare senses were heightened.

The week started with a couple of discouraging emails after Sunday's sermon. Normally, that just comes with the territory—it happens. But these felt really pointed, and to be honest, unfair. Later in the week, I was speaking on campus at Clemson University and my flight out of Waco was delayed—so long that I was going to miss my connection in Dallas. So, I got in the car and drove the ninety miles north to Dallas, parked at the airport, and ran to catch my flight. I made it onto the plane, and the pilot said we were going to have to wait to take off because the plane was out of fuel. At this point, I was starting to wonder if I was going to make it to South Carolina in time to preach that night.

As we were sitting on the tarmac, the woman across the aisle from me started making this strange noise. The woman in front of her turned around and asked if she was okay, but she was unresponsive. I tapped on her shoulder a little bit, but she wouldn't wake up, and I realized this was really serious. I called the flight attendant and she started to check her over.

The flight attendant could not find a pulse, so she asked me to help lay the woman down on the floor so a nurse on board (seated right behind me) could do CPR. I lifted her arms and started to move her out of her seat. While I was lifting her, she woke up and stared at me in a daze. We helped her back into her seat and, once the original fog wore off, we found out she had gone into diabetic shock.

We finally landed at the Greenville, South Carolina, airport, where I had rental car problems (of course). When that was finally sorted out, I jumped in the car and headed to Clemson. I was cutting it close, but I would make it on time and get to preach at this event. I was excited, but I also felt the urgency and the weight of speaking in the middle of Clemson's campus. I also saw some random lightning strikes, which usually does not bode well for an outdoor event. I called the people putting on the event and asked if they had seen the weather. "Yeah, it's heat lightning," they said. "There is no rain in the forecast—like 0 percent chance of rain." So I shrugged it off and carried on.

The time came for me to speak, and we gathered in the middle of the campus in their huge amphitheater that seats two thousand people. It was completely full of college students worshiping their hearts out. It was a holy moment, and I was about to share the gospel. But when I opened my eyes, the sky was filled with dark clouds encircling the stage, and lightning started flickering. It all felt really . . . spiritual. Someone went up to introduce me, said a prayer, said "Amen," and as I walked up, a drop of rain hit my arm. Then, I kid you not, in a matter of seconds, the sky opened up and a torrential downpour fell on this campus.

People started scrambling and running to their cars, the event was canceled, and those putting on the event were rushing to get the soundboard, LED walls, and all the other equipment covered and back inside. All the while I was thinking, *We have got to get this message in front of the students. The Enemy does not want them to hear this message.*

As you might expect, all of this left me with questions. Was the Enemy behind the troubling emails? What about the delayed flight? Were the storms between Texas and South Carolina sent by him? What about the woman on the plane? Did the Enemy put her into a diabetic shock? And the storm at Clemson. It came out of nowhere, right as a couple thousand people were about to hear the gospel.

This felt like more than just a bad week or a funk. It felt deliberate. If the thief does indeed come to "steal, kill, and destroy" (John 10:10) as we discussed earlier in the book, this sure felt like he and his army were out to take a sledgehammer to everything I was trying to do that week. But is that really how this works?

WHAT WE CAN KNOW (AND WHAT WE CAN'T)

Here's the difficulty with everything I just told you—and for that matter, a book about spiritual warfare: There is a limit to how much we can know with 100 percent certainty. And we *crave* certainty.

Some people love certainty more than others, but no one wants to live devoid of finite knowledge and details. We love knowing how the world fits together, and the spiritual realm is no different. We particularly want to know what's going on when it feels like we are directly under some kind of demonic attack. We want to know exactly the kinds of things Satan can and can't do.

At the end of the day, there is a ceiling on how certain we can be. But we can, to the very best of our ability and to the extent that our intellect can take us, look at what the God-inspired Scriptures say, and glean from it all that we can to build a hypothesis. After studying spiritual warfare, here is where I have landed (and I believe Scripture supports this): Satan and his army of demonic forces can do *anything*, yet *only* what God allows. There is no greater example of that in Scripture than the story of Job.

Job is one of the earliest-written books in the Old Testament, and it's a really interesting window into the spiritual realm. You know how some movies have scenes where you can look into another realm, dimension, or world? That is essentially what the story of Job is. We get a glimpse into the spiritual realm as God, the Creator of the heavens and the earth, has a conversation with Satan, the Prince of Darkness. They openly talk, negotiate, and discuss, and God ultimately grants Satan *permission* to test Job, a righteous man who loved and pursued God.

Let's start with the interaction between God and Satan.

One day the angels came to present themselves before the Lord, and Satan also came with them. The Lord said to Satan, "Where have you come from?"

Satan answered the Lord, "From roaming throughout the earth, going back and forth on it."

Then the Lord said to Satan, "Have you considered my servant Job? There is no one on earth like him; he is blameless and upright, a man who fears God and shuns evil."

"Does Job fear God for nothing?" Satan replied. "Have you not put a hedge around him and his household and everything he has? You have blessed the work of his hands, so that his flocks and herds are spread throughout the land. But now stretch out your hand and strike everything he has, and he will surely curse you to your face."

The LORD said to Satan, "Very well, then, everything he has is in your power, but on the man himself do not lay a finger."

Then Satan went out from the presence of the LORD. (1:6–12)

The first chapter of Job is just one giant interpretive challenge. As you read this, it feels like God said, "Hey, Satan, what's up?" Satan said, "Not much, just hanging out on earth." And then God said, "You should mess with Job. He's a good guy. Do something about that." If that's what it feels like to you, you're not crazy, but there was more going on here than meets the eye. God summoned Satan (which is interesting). So, Satan showed up with angels. He had some sort of access to God at God's request.

When God asked Satan where he had been, in the original Hebrew, it's more like God was asking what Satan had been doing. And Satan's response was not, "Hey, I have just been roaming throughout the earth." It's more like, "I'm causing trouble because that is *what I do*. I am stirring up trouble." Satan was boasting about just how disruptive he'd been on the earth. But God reminded him, "You haven't destroyed Job. In fact, you could learn a thing or two from him. Because he faithfully follows Me."

Satan, the accuser, told God that Job didn't love Him, he just loved all the stuff God had given him. "Job has a great life!" Satan said. "If You remove those blessings he's going to turn on You. Just watch!" That's what the accuser does; he accuses. So, Satan went out to test his hypothesis that if Job were to lose everything, he would no longer follow his God.

Spoiler alert: Job loses everything. I mean *everything*. One by one these bearers of bad news came up to Job to tell him what he had lost. He lost oxen, donkeys, sheep, and camels. His servants were killed. And as if that wasn't bad enough, his ten children died tragically. The text tells us that after hearing this news, Job got up and tore his robe and shaved his head. Then he fell to the ground in worship and said: "'Naked I came from my mother's womb, and naked I will depart. The LORD gave and the LORD has taken away; may the name of the LORD be praised.' In all this, Job did not sin by charging God with wrongdoing" (1:21–22).

Can you imagine? Contextualize it for a second: Imagine Job was a member of your church and he showed up on a Sunday morning. His week looked like Chapter 11 bankruptcy with somebody coming to repo everything he owned. There was a fire, and his ranch was destroyed; all the animals were gone. There was no insurance policy, and to make matters worse, in the midst of the fire, all his children were hanging out playing Monopoly around the table when the house burned down with them in it. And then Sunday rolls around and he says, "I will go, and I will worship. Blessed be the name of the Lord." It's otherworldly what's happening to Job in this passage.

WHO CAN SHAKE THE EARTH?

This story can be disconcerting for the reader. Job was a righteous guy! And he lost *everything*. This was not a situation where Job's sin caught up with him and he had to deal with the consequences of his own actions. These things just . . . happened. It makes us start to feel a little more vulnerable and wonder, *What other destruction out there is the result of Satan?* Well, I have an example.

If you don't know much about Haiti's history, you may not know that their former president Jean-Bertrand Aristide dedicated the nation to the practice of voodoo (and Satan).[1] You're probably thinking, *Why would he ever do that?* It is a fair question, and one that I asked on a trip I took there. The answer was fascinating. The man I asked said, "We believe in God; we just think He's slow. And voodoo is fast. Satan operates quicker than God does." So because of President Aristide's actions, large swaths of people turned toward a man-made religion in hopes that it would solve their problems.

When I visited Haiti, I saw voodoo temples everywhere I went, and it seemed as though there was a voodoo priest, or two or three, in every village. It was common to see a church on one corner and across the street a voodoo temple with witch doctors you could turn to and bargain with to try to find healing.

In 2010, a gigantic earthquake hit Haiti. It was utterly devastating. Millions of people were affected. Hundreds of thousands of homes and buildings were destroyed. While no one knows exactly how many lives were lost, the Haitian government's estimate placed it over 300,000 people.[2] After the earthquake hit, there was a great revival in Haiti. Some prominent Christian pastors in the US declared that this was God's judgment on Haiti for turning its back on Him. Churches were filled with people. People were turning back to God. I had the opportunity to visit after the earthquake and the people I talked with said, "We believe Satan has power, but he's not strong enough to shake the earth." Christians heard that and said, "Yeah, that's right!"

But if you hold that up against the story of Job you might say, "Well, hold on. He actually *is* strong enough to shake the earth."

He can do just about anything God lets him do. He can shake the earth, he can send storms, wind, tornadoes, hurricanes, wildfires . . . anywhere you see chaos and destruction, he's been. There's a lot he *can* do.

You see, the world is not how God originally intended it to be. His will is for us to be in right relationship with Him. Going back to the garden of Eden, we see how humans have a desire to go our own way and do our own thing, and our desire to sin left a fracture in the world. So, the world we have now has cancer and heartbreak and pain and divorce and death and disease. Destruction. This is what we're left with.

This is also the answer to the age-old question of *why* these terrible things happen. When tornadoes come and destruction takes place and you ask the question, "Well, is Satan behind *that*?" the answer is: Anywhere on earth where we see destruction, Satan is behind it—either directly or indirectly—because the world is fallen. In God's original plan, His first and best desire would not be that people die in tornadoes, or hurricanes, or tsunamis, or earthquakes, or fires.

But here we are in the second-best, and we don't know exactly how the Enemy is behind it. Say an arsonist sets a house on fire, and that one house fire ends up burning down the whole neighborhood. What destruction is the arsonist responsible for? The simple answer is *all of it*. And so, in all the destruction of the Enemy, we feel a wake of destruction. We don't know if it's direct or indirect— a peripheral consequence or a direct attack. We probably won't be able to sort that out on this side of eternity. But any pain, any suffering, and any destruction we experience under the sun, he is behind.

We must reconcile that God could stop it. He can. And so, why wouldn't He?

OPPORTUNITIES TO TRUST

Each one of these moments—when the disaster strikes, when the loss happens, when the diagnosis is given—presents us with the opportunity to either trust God or not. Think about it this way: If life were exclusively rainbows and butterflies, you would not need faith. The biggest thing God wants from you is faith. He wants you to trust Him. And each one of these moments is an opportunity for you to grow your faith.

When my oldest daughter, Presley (the lollipop girl), was just above the toddler age, she went to swimming lessons. I remember her walking out with shaky knees on the diving board, and me treading water in the deep end with my hands out saying, "Jump! Jump! Come on, Presley! You can do it! Jump!" Now, what was she thinking as a three- or four-year-old? *Well, I guess my daddy wants me to drown now. He's going to let me drown.* Of course not! I was saying, "No! I'm not going to let you drown! Jump! You can do it! You can do it!" But when you are on that diving board and you begin to trust your senses, it seems like you are being asked to jump and drown.

When you are in the thick of it, it is disorienting. When a baby has died in a womb or your life has been flipped on its head, it is hard to make sense of it all. Maybe someone who promised amazing things to you has now broken that trust or someone you love is hit with a disease or suffering. When you are sitting in that grief and in that pain and you are looking to God, you might think, *God, You're asking me to drown.*

But God is saying here, "No, no, no. I am asking you to trust Me. I can bring good from anything, in ways no one else can."

Hear me out on this: You will never get in a bind believing that God can make good from anything.

Reread that sentence, highlight it, underline it—whatever you need to do to make that thought stick. You will *often* get in a bind when you start telling Him the good He needs to bring—when you start telling Him, "No, this is the good I want!" God wants you to relinquish your desire to be God and to trust Him. Even when you feel as though taking that leap of faith off the diving board is more than you can do.

If you fast-forward to the end of Job's story, you will see how God brought it full circle. The Bible says in Job 42:12, "The LORD blessed the latter part of Job's life more than the former part." The Scriptures say Job received twice as much as he had before, and he had ten more children, and his daughters were known throughout the land as the most beautiful women on earth. And it just goes on and on about the ways that the Lord blessed him.

Here is my hunch. When you get into heaven and you find Job, he is not going to be in some tiny shack. That would be a confusing ending for a man who remained so faithful. He is probably going to have the biggest house on the hill. As you are getting your heaven tour you will say, "Who lives *there*?"

"Oh, that's Job."

"Oh yeah, I read about him—forty-two grueling chapters. I cannot understand how he survived that."

Then you find Job! And when you start talking to him you say, "Job, tell me how you did it. How did you endure that?"

"Endure what?"

"When you lost everything. Remember? When you lost all the thousands of heads of cattle and your children died, you were covered in boils . . ."

"Oh gosh, I forgot about that. I haven't thought about that in several thousand years, actually. How'd you know that? Oh, it's in a book? Okay, gotcha. Man, that's interesting. Nah, like, the Lord made good on that. I don't know if you noticed what He has blessed me with up here forever and ever and ever and ever, but I am good. He gives and takes away."

You need to know that just like Job, whose second part of life was better than the first, your next life is going to be infinitely better than the first. In this life you will have trouble, but take heart; Jesus has overcome the world (John 16:33).

When I think back on that night in Clemson when my speaking opportunity was rained out by an unforeseen thunderstorm, I remember feeling really discouraged at first. Did I really travel hundreds of miles just to be introduced before the skies opened up? I felt like God wanted those students to hear the gospel, so the leadership team and I huddled up and decided to use technology as our friend. We challenged the students to join us on Instagram live at 9:00 p.m. and to help us spread the word. That night as we went live, more than five thousand people tuned in to watch (more than twice as many fit in the amphitheater). When the Enemy tried to bring destruction, God provided an alternative way. God works to undo the destruction caused by the Enemy.

MAKE IT STICK: JOURNAL IT

Think back on a time in your life when you felt like you were facing spiritual warfare. When did you experience a series of challenges and obstacles that seemed beyond normal coincidence?

Write a couple of paragraphs (or put all your thoughts in bullet-point form) about the situation. What were you feeling? Did you feel like the Enemy was specifically targeting you? How did you see God working amid the difficulty? Did the situation change your perspective on spiritual warfare or trusting God during a challenging time?

CHAPTER 5

THE VILLAIN DISTRACTS

ANY TIME OUR FAMILY GOES ON A ROAD TRIP, THE same plotline plays out time and time again. We will inevitably stop to get gas, and when we do, Monica will ask me to get her a bottle of water when I go inside. I'll pump the gas, go inside, and immediately get distracted once I'm in there. I usually have a few texts or emails to respond to while I walk through the parking lot, and once I'm inside it's like the whole world is at my fingertips.

Mesmerized by the walls of drinks, I ponder what I want. Sometimes I will even grab a few for the kids, because I'm a good father like that. Then I'll hit the snack rows. *What do I want today?* Maybe Nerds Gummy Clusters. Maybe pistachios. Maybe chips. Beef jerky? It all depends on what I'm in the mood for that day. Once I make the final selections I head to the checkout, about to drop thirty dollars on gas station snacks, because I cannot help myself.

When I get out to the car and pass out everyone's rations for the next leg of the journey, Monica will ask, "Did you get the bottle of water?" Quickly, my shoulders slump and I realize the one thing I was supposed to get in the first place is still inside, because I got distracted. I will then trudge back into the store, grab the water, pay, and then we're on our way once again.

As I think about how the villain tries to destroy us in the twenty-first century, I can think of no way more common than the weapon of distraction—because we are *so* easily distracted. Just ask anyone who has parented a small child. From a young age, we are easily thrown off task. There's no telling how many times I've asked my kids to do a simple task, like brushing their teeth or changing their clothes, only to find them ten minutes later glued to the TV, or scrolling on their phone, or plotting to buy something else they don't need. As we get older, the variables change (maybe), but the principle does not.

I once met with a pastor who had returned from twenty years of serving as a missionary in Russia. He met with our church staff, and as we were talking, I asked, "So, what did you notice about America? What have you noticed that has changed here?" Honestly, I am not sure what answer I was expecting, but the first thing he said was definitely not on my top-hundred list of possible answers.

"Storage buildings."

"What?" I responded, confused.

He continued, "It seems like every road I drive on there are huge rows of garage doors. Sometimes they're even stacked on top of each other into the sky. There are these big buildings with garage doors. You guys have really doubled down on storage buildings since I left. I thought people put their stuff in their houses?"

I explained, "Sometimes they have more stuff than their house can hold, so they rent a storage building."

He said, "Let me get this straight: People build houses for their stuff, but sometimes they have so much stuff it does not fit in their house, so they have to rent a garage off-property to keep their stuff that they do not use but they may again someday."

Bingo.

This world is not our home, but we sure do try to make our home here, don't we? We have so much to be distracted by that we can't even keep it under one roof.

NOT NEW, BUT HEIGHTENED

Distraction is not a new phenomenon, but I do believe it has increased in its intensity in recent years. Think about one of the last instructions Jesus gave His followers before He ascended into heaven. He told them to go and make disciples (Matthew 28:19–20). These are the most famous of all last words. We even have a name for them: the Great Commission! Jesus was saying, "Hey guys, I want you to take everything you have seen and learned from Me and pass it on to other people."

The instructions for us are no different. Almost two thousand years later, His expectations are still the same: We are to believe and follow all Jesus did and said, and teach others to do the same. But today there is so much to take our eyes off what is important. The disciples didn't have to compete with TikTok, select sports, or a rise-and-grind corporate work culture. The disciples weren't up against the suburbs, college football, and 401(k)s.

Back when we called it Twitter, I remember seeing a tweet from John Piper that stopped me dead in my tracks. He wrote, "One of the great uses of Twitter and Facebook will be to prove at the Last Day that prayerlessness was not from lack of time."[1] You can't really argue with the point he's making. (Well, I'm sure some-one would argue with him because it's the internet, after all.) But he is spot-on in his analysis. There is simply so much out there for us to pay attention to. And anything the Enemy can use to distract us from the mission we have been given is a success in his book.

Do you understand what I'm saying? You're not just distracted. You are being distracted strategically by the one who seeks to keep you from the pleasures of God. He's dangling all the world has to offer in an effort to appeal to your worldly desires. And for so many people, he is incredibly successful.

And what's at stake here? Honestly, the future of the world. Jesus' commission compels us to go and make disciples. One reason we don't do this is that we are so distracted with our lives, our classes, our work, our families, and our conflicts. We—and I'm talking about the church (particularly the Western church)—don't spend enough time focusing on the life of Jesus, so that we might emulate it for others.

What does it look like to focus our lives on following Jesus?

Honestly, it's a fight. I tell my church this, and I will share this with you as well: Sometimes when I teach or write, I feel like the Spirit is at work in my life and is allowing me to say, "Follow me on this issue as I follow Christ, and let's all grow together." Other times, I feel like I'm learning and wrestling and growing right alongside everyone else. Spiritual warfare is one of those concepts for me that I feel like I'm learning in real time.

Even while writing this, it's a struggle for me to not let the villain win in this part of my life. I, like many of you, have a calendar constantly telling me where to be and when. It dings or buzzes every time someone reaches out or responds to me. I have a wife and kids who each have their own hobbies, interests, and activities that I am keeping up with. I have external pressures coming at me from every angle, and sometimes I feel like I can barely keep up with what's being asked of me.

Now, that's not me trying to throw a pity party. That's just me telling you I get it, and we're in the same boat. The more I have studied and prepared for this book, the more I am convinced that one of the Enemy's favorite tools to lower the effectiveness of believers is to put distractions in front of them that will divert their focus elsewhere. But another trick is to make people busy with religious activities, under the guise of Christianity, to make them feel like they're part of a movement when they are really just going through the motions.

INOCULATED TO THE FAITH

In his book *Celebration of Discipline*, Richard Foster says, "In contemporary society our Adversary majors in three things: noise, hurry, and crowds. If he can keep us engaged in 'muchness' and 'manyness,' he will rest satisfied."[2] When I read that, I can't help but think about my life right before I started following Jesus, and even those early years when I was a Christian but the world still had a pull on my heart.

When I went to church I'd sit in the very back row. I'd hear the message and think, *Oh man, that's good. That was a good message. That one was convicting.* Then I'd walk out the doors of the church and get in my Jaguar with the black leather and the navigation system (I'm talking the early 1.0 version of navigation systems). I'd drive it to my condo, which was on the top floor of a high-rise building that overlooked downtown Dallas, balcony and all. I'd put on a suit and go to work downtown. Everything was *good.* The car, the condo, the job. I was busy, and busyness seemed *good.* You know, B-U-S-Y. Being. Under. Satan's. Yoke. *BUSY.*

I had all these responsibilities and obligations, and I had to work hard to pay for all my toys and trinkets and . . . what was that message at church again? I remember it was . . . good. Was it something about Jesus? The Bible? Was it Hosea? Was it Habakkuk?

Hezekiah? Is there even a Hezekiah? I could never remember, but it was good. But guys: I was distracted. I looked like a Christian. I smelled like a Christian. I could even talk like a Christian. But I was so consumed by the world. The world had a grip on my heart that I did not want to give up.

I think so many of us fall into a trap where we want to run this race called life hard and fast. We have to keep it all up, keep the mortgage paid, make sure the car is paid for, and do our very best to keep up with the Joneses (whoever they are). We're going to trip over the finish line called retirement, and we're going to die in our sleep someday and our kids are going to enjoy our stuff.

That's the kind of person I like to call the consumed Christian. This is the person who is so consumed with the world that they cannot rightfully respond to the gospel. This person appears to have it all together. They have the car you want, the house you want. Their kids are smarter than yours. They have the bumper sticker to prove it. Speaking of bumper stickers, they've run marathons and are always running circles around you in life. These people are in church all the time—even more than you! But these people are distracted by the world. I like to say it like this: They are *inoculated* to Christianity.

Inoculated is the word we use for someone who has received a vaccine. We receive just enough of a disease to build up antibodies so we can't catch the real version. When we're inoculated to Christianity, we hear the gospel over and over and think, *Yeah, yeah. Jesus died for my sins. God raised Him from the dead. Easter, put on the fancy dress, hunt for eggs. Easter, take the picture. Christmas, let's go. Presents and the nativity scene, got it. Jesus was born in a manger, grew up, died for my sins, got it.* But there is no response with joy! There is no emotion, there is no movement. Nothing changes. It's like we are confronted with this mind-blowing reality that Jesus saved us from death and destruction and we respond with, "So what?" We have heard the truth so many times that it's not exciting for us and it doesn't lead to a true heart change. The villain in your story loves this! He doesn't even mind that we go to church because he uses our church hobby to keep us from following Jesus.

WHAT'S YOUR GOLDEN CALF?

There is a fascinating story in Exodus 32 where Moses went up to the top of a mountain to convene with God. While he was gone, the people got tired of waiting. They just assumed Moses was not coming back, so they went to Aaron (the second-in-command) and told him they should form some new gods instead since Moses had vanished. Aaron didn't even put up a fight, but instead told them to bring all their jewelry so they could melt it down and form a new idol, which just so happened to be a golden calf. They did exactly that, and it turned into a *party.*

God became furious and told Moses what had happened. Moses was able to convince God to relent and not punish them right away, and then he left. When he saw the party below, he was so frustrated that he threw the tablets with the Law on them that he had carried down the mountain. He then confronted Aaron, who told him how they ended up in this predicament, all while the people reveled around him.

At first when you read it, you think, *How could they do that? How could they be so dumb?* But it is not all that dumb. They simply got bored and tired of waiting on God (and Moses) to act, so they took matters into their own hands. The distraction led them to do something God had made it really clear *not* to do.

We are still crafting our own gods (little *g*) today. We think about our jobs, our houses, our spouses, our kids, and we have a lot of things going on, so we compartmentalize our faith to nothing outside of a Sunday checklist. We think, *I'll go on Sundays and I'll have a little bit of chicken soup for the soul, get that shot in the arm. I'll get those words of encouragement so I can get through the week and get busy, busy, busy, busy, busy, and do it all over again.* And the gospel takes the backseat of our lives. It does not belong there. It should be the car and the road and the destination. It is everything. There's no compartmentalization in Christianity.

This fragmented thinking leads us to a false, unbiblical version of Christianity. It's hobby Christianity. Real Christianity—when you have truly encountered Jesus—changes everything. It influences how you date, who you marry, how you love your spouse, how you parent, how you work, what you say, how you dress, where you go, what you purchase . . . it influences all of that. But how do we begin to live that way? It starts with a clear mind.

WHY YOU NEED A SOBER MIND

Multiple times throughout the book of 1 Peter, Peter (the same one who walked alongside Jesus, denied Him, and ultimately went on to be one of the most zealous evangelists ever) instructed the recipients of his letter to be of sober mind. While we typically read the word *sober* and immediately think of alcohol, Peter was calling believers to a life of being clear-minded.

In his commentary on 1 Peter, pastor Juan R. Sanchez explains it like this:

> When we think of the word "sober," we think of it in the context of alcohol. That provides a helpful framework. Consider how drunkenness affects every aspect of the human body. It clouds our judgment; it slows our reflexes; it provokes us to do

things we would not normally do. . . . Peter speaks of the mind not merely as the source of intellectual activity; for Peter, it is the mind that determines or controls our actions. He is talking about mental preparedness and resolve; disciplined thinking that will control right behavior. In this sense, "self-control" is also a good translation.[3]

Alcohol, like all the other temptations and distractions of this world, will amuse and entertain you, all while making you ineffective for the kingdom of God. It will do the exact *opposite* of making you alert. Peter gave the instruction to "be alert and of sober mind. Your enemy the devil prowls around like a roaring lion looking for someone to devour" (1 Peter 5:8). Here he gave both the *what* and the *why*. The *what* is that we need to be alert and of sober mind.

When I think about that command, I think of all the professions where we need people to be alert and of sober mind. The pilot of every airplane should be alert and sober-minded. The surgeon in every hospital should be alert and sober-minded. Why? Because if they are distracted by anything, the consequences are grave. That's what Peter was trying to get across to his audience. If the Christian is distracted by other things, the consequences are dire.

Then he went on to describe the Enemy as someone prowling around like a roaring lion. Think about the animal metaphors used to describe people throughout Scripture, both in the Old and New Testaments. Do you know what the big one is? We are often described as sheep. David talked about the Lord being his shepherd (Psalm 23). Jesus told a parable about lost sheep (Luke 15). If we are like sheep, but our Enemy is prowling around like a lion, that seems problematic. Did you hear about that time the sheep beat up the lion? Me neither. A lion has never looked at a sheep and thought, *Oh no, what am I going to do?* No. A lion looks at a sheep and thinks, *Dinner is served!*

Sheep wander. Sheep get distracted. Sheep get weighed down by the weight of their own wool, especially in the rain. Sometimes we get so weighed down by the concerns of this world that we can hardly function. We are blinded by the choices we've made. We think we're doing fine, but we are just moments from being devoured by the one who prowls around like a roaring lion.

OUR ONLY AIM

Living an undistracted life sounds great in theory, right? But how do we actually live this way? My hunch is that nobody is going to raise their hand and say, "Actually, JP, I love when the Enemy distracts me and takes me off mission." Culture is working against us. Technology is working against us. The Enemy is constantly finding ways to give our brains all the dopamine hits it can possibly give us to keep us glued to our favorite devices.

It seems like there are two competing schools of thought when it comes to trying to eliminate distractions. In AD 529 a monk named Benedict of Nursia founded multiple monasteries and put all his thoughts down into what's known as Benedict's Rule.[4] Basically, Benedict advocated that devotion to God could best be achieved by withdrawing from society and focusing on prayer, study, and work alongside his fellow monastic brethren. This has been emulated by other groups throughout the years, but the basic premise is the same: If you cut off *all* the outside distractions, you will be better able to connect with God.

But wait: What about carrying out the Great Commission, making disciples, letting our light shine before others, and the whole idea of being in the world but not of it that we are taught so often in Christian circles? We can't take the escapism route, can we? But if we're living in the world like everybody else, will we not just keep finding ourselves in this cycle of distraction right where the Enemy wants us?

As I wrestle through this in my own life (and trust me—it is a wrestle), a verse continuously comes to mind from Acts 20, where the apostle Paul was preparing to board a ship bound for Jerusalem. It was time for him to leave the Ephesians—his close friends that he had served alongside and a church he cared deeply for—to head to a place where he knew the authorities wanted to imprison him. He knew this was his last chance to say goodbye to the people and place he loved so dearly. We get a glimpse into his farewell speech, where he said this in verse 24:

> I consider my life worth nothing to me; my only aim is to finish the race and complete the task the Lord Jesus has given me— the task of testifying to the good news of God's grace.

Why not stay in the place where he was safe, comfortable, and well cared for? Paul knew the next step of obedience in his life was to get on that ship. He wanted to complete the task he had been given and continue "testifying to the good news of God's grace," even if it meant risking everything. Because that's what it meant to complete the task Jesus had given him.

It's so easy for us to get distracted by everything that's happening all around us. Even *good* things can take our eyes off the *main* task Jesus has called us to complete. And it's hard. I've seen the Enemy distract friends over the years who take their eyes off their task. They get caught up in disagreements or the wrong pursuits. Their aim shifts—at first ever so slightly, and then all of a sudden they are aiming at a completely different target.

My son has recently taken an interest in hunting. Just the

other day we were at my mom's house in the country sighting in his scope. This means we had to adjust the crosshairs in the scope so the rifle would send a bullet to anything it was aimed at. We aimed at a target, fired a bullet, and looked closely where it hit. If it was high, we would adjust the scope down. If it was to the right, we would adjust the scope left. We did this until it would consistently hit whatever it was aiming at. While Paul had never fired a gun, this illustration is helpful to us as we think through how to aim every single day. And what is the target we are aiming for? Faithfulness. Every. Single. Day.

If we wake up tomorrow and declare that we are done letting the Enemy distract us and it will never happen again, my hunch is that we will all go to bed discouraged. I wish it were that easy, but unfortunately it's not. But I do believe if we start our day asking God, "What does faithfulness look like today? In this meeting? In this class? In this conversation?" He will aid us in that effort. We just have to make sure we are aiming at the right target and leaving distraction behind.

MAKE IT STICK: DISTRACTION JOURNAL

For the next seventy-two hours, keep a log of all the things you are distracted by. Then, with the help of a group or a few individuals who can keep you accountable, craft a plan to start removing the distractions from your life that the Enemy is using to take you off course.

Pro-tip: Start with the Screen Time report on your devices, which keeps track of how much time you spend using them. What would it take for you to cut that time in half this week?

CHAPTER 6

THE VILLAIN DECEIVES

IT'S NO SECRET THAT I HAVE RUN WITH THE wrong crowds in some seasons of my life. In my pre-Jesus days, I fell in with all kinds of the wrong people. In one particular season in high school, I ran with some guys who stole things. Now, these guys were not master criminals pulling off *Ocean's Eleven* kind of stunts, but they would steal things. We would go into a gas station or Walmart and they would find something they wanted. They would wear a puffy, oversized coat (which should have been the sign we were up to no good in South Texas), slip the items inside their coats, and walk out the door.

Now, I couldn't bring myself to do that. Before you think too highly of me, it is not because I was righteous, but because I was a coward. I was afraid of getting caught. I could play out the scenario in my head. As I said earlier, my dad was this John Wayne–like, larger-than-life kind of man. Do you know what my dad had no patience for? Me engaging in petty theft and ruining the family name in our small town.

As a teenager, the worst-case scenario for me was getting caught by store security and the cops being called and then my dad finding out. The idea of a cop calling my dad and saying, "Mr. Pokluda, we need you to come down to the station and pick up your son," was enough for me to draw a line in the sand. My moral compass was not all that strong, but I had a healthy fear of my dad.

The one thing I would do, which is still *very much* stealing, was switch the price tags. I would take the price tag of something not worth very much and put it on something of great value. One hot summer night we went to the store and I saw the Boyz II Men CD I had been wanting, and it was $13.99. The problem was that I, with no job and no income, didn't have $13.99. So, I looked around the store to make sure no employees were around.

My friends knew what I was up to, so they served as lookouts (just in case). About ten feet away there was a bin full of movie theater candy boxes that were all one dollar, so I grabbed one of those boxes, moved the price tag from the candy box to the CD, and all of a sudden, I was well on my way to being the owner of a brand-new CD. The cashier would ring it up, think nothing of it other than *Wow, that kid just got a great deal*, and I would leave with it.

This is another way to say, I stole stuff too. It was deceptive. It was theft. And for the record, I have made that right since then. Still, at that time in my life, deception came a little too naturally.

THE OLDEST TRICK IN THE BOOK

My hunch is, the reason I was so comfortable living a life of deception at that time is that deception is a tool of the Enemy. The Scriptures make it clear that one of the Enemy's primary methods of attack is deception. Satan *lies*—trying to convince us of all sorts of falsehoods.

In my years before becoming a follower of Jesus and receiving the Holy Spirit, it made perfect sense that I was content leading people astray. People like I was, according to 2 Corinthians 11:13–15, "are false apostles, deceitful workers, masquerading as apostles of Christ. And no wonder, for Satan himself masquerades as an angel of light. It is not surprising, then, if his servants also masquerade as servants of righteousness." Satan and his forces disguise themselves as the "good guys" as another means of deception. They try to make what is evil look good. They are switching the price tags to deceive us, and make what is valuable seem less valuable.

Jesus said to those persecuting Him, "You belong to your father, the devil, and you want to carry out your father's desires. He was a murderer from the beginning, not holding to the truth, for there is no truth in him. When he lies, he speaks his native language, for he is a liar and the father of lies" (John 8:44). How does the devil lie? To be honest, we don't exactly know. In the spiritual realm, thoughts take some sort of different dimension and capacity. And so, we don't exactly know *how* he gets the lies to us. We just know his lies are very simple. And they are almost constant.

Most likely, lying is his primary method of attack, because he has been doing it since the beginning of creation. He lies. And what is his primary lie? It is one you still believe. Honestly, you're probably going to believe it today at some point, if you haven't already. This lie has two facets: (1) God is not good, and (2) you can't trust God.

This is the first play out of the playbook Satan runs in Genesis 3. Think about that story: God had created the world, all the animals, all the birds, the sun, the moon, the sky, the ocean, the land . . . all of it. And it was all perfect. Then He created Adam and

Eve, in His image, and tasked them with ruling over the earth with one explicit instruction: Do not, under any circumstance, eat from the Tree of the Knowledge of Good and Evil because if you do, you will die. Then Satan, who the text describes as "crafty," scurried over to Eve and got her to doubt God: *Did God really say that?*

Eve knew exactly what God had said! She even quoted it back to the serpent. Then the Enemy doubled down with a lie, saying, "You will not certainly die . . . For God knows that when you eat from it your eyes will be opened, and you will be like God, knowing good and evil" (Genesis 3:4–5). He was not only questioning what God said, but now he was downright refuting it.

Once everything came into the light and their sin was exposed (and it always is), Eve told God in Genesis 3:13 that "the serpent deceived me." In that moment, the entire course of humanity changed. One act of deception from the Enemy and Adam and Eve were forced from the garden of Eden. Ever since that moment, Satan and his forces have been using the tactic of deception to make us question the goodness of God.

Today, this plays out in our lives in a number of ways. It is (likely) not happening to you as a serpent coming up and whispering in your ear; it is most likely happening at the thought level. The Enemy *loves* to mess with your thoughts. Remember: There is a demonic spirit out there who is studying you and knows how to mess with your head. Think about the lies the Enemy feeds you:

God is ripping you off. Why has He not given you a spouse? It seems like everyone else has one. Oh, and you do not need to wait until you are married to have sex. Why would God not want you to have fun? Oh, you don't get to live in that neighborhood? Your kids don't get to go to that school? Oh, poor you. You're stuck married to him? Everything he does is so annoying. Just bail out of that; you would be happier that way.

Satan is doing what he does best: sneaking up and affecting your thoughts, saying, "You got ripped off. You got dealt a bad hand."

This is the oldest trick in the book: to call what is evil good and what is good evil. He takes things of infinite worth and he makes them look cheap. And he takes things that are cheap, and temporarily pleasurable, and makes them look luxurious and eternal. He is like me at Walmart in junior high. Taking the price tag of a CD and putting it on a CD player. Satan takes the price tag of a healthy marriage and switches it with a one-night stand. He makes marriage look undesirable and sex outside of marriage look very desirable. And all of us, at times, have bought one of his lies. We have been duped before and will be again. We have been led astray.

A common question people ask is, "Can he read my mind?" I believe he and his forces cannot read your mind in a traditional sense. He is not omnipotent (all-powerful). He is not God. I don't believe that he has some kind of X-ray vision into your mind where he can peek in and know everything you are thinking. So, in a traditional sense, he cannot read your mind. If it were that simple, he would have been able to read Job's mind and see if Job was going to turn from God or not. But God could read Job's mind, and God could see his heart. God knows the future. He knows how that's going to go, but Satan doesn't.

But here is a disclaimer: I *do* believe he can read your mind in a different sense. Here is an example: sometimes when I am talking with Monica, I'll say, "How do you feel about this situation?" She'll say, "I don't know how I feel right now." Then I'll say, "Well, it seems like you feel this, this, this, and this." And she'll say, "That is *exactly* how I feel. I just was unable to put it into words."

Why can I do that? Because I have studied her. I have committed to understanding how her mind works. In the same way,

Satan (or some demon) has studied you and understands how you think, what trips you up, what will take you out. He did it with your great-great-great-grandparent. He's been lying to generations of your family. His angels know where you're vulnerable, what you like, and what makes you very angry. They cannot force the believer to think something, but they can lie to you. They can influence your thoughts, and this is why the truth is so important.

WHAT THE ACCUSER DOES

The Enemy is also described in the Bible as *the accuser*. Revelation 12:9 describes him as someone who "leads the whole world astray." The very next verse says that he accuses God's people day and night. But accuses them of what, exactly?

The more I have studied this and spent time thinking about it, the more I believe this can happen in two ways. One is the way that probably popped into your mind: It is like the Enemy is hovering behind you and flooding your mind with the reminders you are not good enough. Every time you lose your temper, drink that, smoke that, click on that hashtag—whatever it is for you—and you feel that conviction of the Spirit and you want to repent, there is the Enemy ready to pounce, saying, "You did it again. You are the worst. Are you sure God really loves you? Does anyone love you? And you call yourself a Christian." Accusation after accusation after accusation. You feel beat up and attacked. That is the accuser, doing what the accuser does.

This is the reason so many Christians live lives of isolation, shame, and guilt. The Enemy *loves* when we keep our mess in the dark. The accuser *loves* for you to feel like you are the only one struggling with a certain sin, and that you cannot or should not tell people about it. Some of you reading this right now have things in your past (or even right now) that you think you're going to take to the grave. You say, "That's an aspect of my life I'm going to continue to hide from people because if they knew that thing about me, they would reject me." Some of the usual suspects are abortion, abuse, addiction, and sexual perversion or desires.

I understand the desire to keep that a secret because I *was* that person as I sat on the back row in a church with a pounding headache from a night of partying. I was thinking, *These people in their Sunday best, they can't relate to me!* And that is right where the Enemy wants us to stay forever and ever—with secrets. The Scriptures call us to walk in the light and be children of the light (1 John 1:7–9) and to confess our sins to one another and be healed (James 5:16). Whenever we feel tempted to keep "that thing" in the dark, that's not of the Spirit. That's the accuser out to deceive us and pull us away from the truth of the Scriptures.

There is another way Satan lives up to his title of accuser. He manipulates people to accuse believers of evil, even when there's nothing evil actually going on. In preparation for this book, I experienced this in my own life. One Monday morning I got two different emails with two different accusations about things that I'd said (or technically did *not* say) in that Sunday's sermon. I was confident of what I had said, but I went back and watched the recordings from the day before just to make sure I wasn't losing my mind. Sure enough, the accusations were without merit. So why did that happen?

In 1 Peter 2:12, Peter implored believers, "Live such good lives among the pagans that, though they accuse you of doing wrong, they may see your good deeds and glorify God on the day he visits us." While Peter was writing this, Nero was the emperor. You can go read his Wikipedia page if you want to, but I will summarize it this way: Nero was a wicked, wicked man. After Peter wrote this letter, Nero set Rome on fire. People died and houses were destroyed. And Nero basically said, "The Christians did it! Those who follow Jesus, the Way." People then turned on the Christians and began to torture them for sport.

Peter's instructions make it clear that followers of Jesus *will be* accused of all kinds of wrongdoing, even when they have not done anything wrong. I believe that's why Peter was trying to compel his readers to live such good, wholesome, respectable, godly lives that even the pagan nonbelievers around them would know that there was no way the accusations could be true—because they would come to trust the character of the Christians around them.

KNOW THE TRUTH

If the Enemy's tactic from the very beginning has been to deceive and manipulate, it raises the stakes on the importance of knowing what is true. As the decades go by and generations change, the lies of the day start to change too. So what is Satan's latest lie? I am hearing it more and more with each passing year, and it is only gaining steam with my younger friends: "Well, it's *my* truth."

Another way to say it is, "What's your truth?" or "That's their truth." It is the lie of truth being relative. Think about it this way: If my truth is gravity and your truth is weightlessness, and we climb to the tallest building in your city and you jump off, you are going to see that my truth wins out. Right? Because it is the actual truth.

Jesus made a life-altering statement in John 14:6 when He said, "I am the way and the truth and the life. No one comes to the Father except through me." What happens now is people respond and say, "That's great—that is *your* truth. My truth is Brahma (a Hindu god). My truth is Allah (the god of Islam). My truth is fill-in-the-blank god or practice." If we believe the Scriptures are true,

inspired by God, and authoritative, one day we are going ι
and we are going to realize Jesus is exactly who He said He is. Th.
He is the truth, and what He said is true: "you will know the truth,
and the truth will set you free" (John 8:32).

Friends, for the rest of your life remember this: The way you
fight a lie is with the truth. Whoever knows the truth wins. And
there are two truths that I want you to have a death grip on today.
First is the gospel. Jesus paid the price for our sins. He died for
them on the cross, and He was raised from the dead. He defeated
death, giving us hope for eternal life, so we can be with God
forever—not because of what we do, but because of what He did
for us. This is the first truth, and it is one we can't just blow past.
If we grasp the gospel truth, it changes everything.

The second truth is that we can trust the instructions in the
Bible. Second Timothy 3:16 says, "All Scripture is God-breathed
and is useful for teaching, rebuking, correcting and training in
righteousness." The Bible isn't just some old dusty book, full of
irrelevant tales. It's the tool God has given us to fight back against
every lie, accusation, and attempt at deception the Enemy will
throw at us.

The Enemy loves when we believe the lie that "our truth" overrides the truth God has given us in His Word. He will dance with
you all day long. That is the equivalent of you pulling up a chair to
your table and saying, "Hey, Satan, have a seat." He says, "Oh, you
have a rebellious spirit against God's Word. Hey guys, I got one
over here!" Some demon will gladly lead you away. Sadly, I have
seen countless people in the body of Christ go their own way, ven-
ture further from the church, and withdraw from God's people, all
because they believed the lie that their truth wins out.

I am not selling you a false bill of goods here. I know that the
truth can change your life. It can revise the script of your story
with which the villain has been deceiving you. We will talk more

about how to fight back against the Enemy's attacks, but when it comes to combatting the Enemy's lies, we must know what is *actually* true. You can't go out unarmed into this battle. Imagine how that would play out. Do you know what he's going to say to you? He will speak to you like this: *You are worthless. Totally worthless.*

Now, if you don't have the Word of God hidden in your heart, it's easy to buy that lie and say, "You're right. I am." But if you are equipped for the moment you can say, "Wait, hold on. I've been created in the image of God (Genesis 1:27). I've been purchased by His blood; He purchased me with His Son. And I've been created in Christ Jesus for a purpose—to do the good works that God has prepared for me to do (Ephesians 2:10). He has a purpose for me. I'm not worthless. That is what the truth says."

The deceiver might continue: *Just take a second look at him. Take a second look at her. I know you guys aren't married. That's okay. Just a second look. It's no big deal. Just entertain the thought. What if?*

"No, Job 31:1 says that 'I made a covenant with my eyes not to look lustfully' at another woman. Matthew 5 says that if I look lustfully at someone, I've already committed adultery with them, and 1 Corinthians 6 says that I am supposed to flee sexual immorality. Because all other sins a person commits are sins outside their body, but whoever sins sexually sins against their own body. I've been bought by the Holy Spirit. I am not my own, so I am going to honor God with my body."

He won't give up with his lies. *You know, if you just had a little bit more. Maybe a little bit more money. If you just lived in that neighborhood, had that car, you'd be happy then. If you just increased your income a little bit, you'd be happy.*

"That's interesting, deceiver, because Scripture tells me that whoever loves money never has enough (Ecclesiastes 5:10). That, in Proverbs 23:5, it sprouts wings and flies away. It says that with food and clothing, I should be content with these (1 Timothy 6:8–10). In fact, it says in 1 Timothy 6 that anyone who loves money falls into temptation, into a trap, and is lured away. So, you're a liar."

Now, if you have never practiced this, you are not going to be very good at it in the beginning. But the Scriptures tell us if we are followers of Jesus Christ and we have His Spirit, He will help us in this effort (John 14:26). We are to take thoughts captive and make them obedient to Christ (2 Corinthians 10:5). This is a continual, tiresome effort. I have met with lots of people who've said, "I can't do this." Really what they are saying in most cases is they have given up too easily. I encourage you to not stop short of success, which is exactly what the Enemy wants you to do.

The author of Hebrews said, "In your struggle against sin, you have not yet resisted to the point of shedding your blood" (12:4). So keep fighting! Don't give up! Start today. Let the truth win out.

MAKE IT STICK: LOGGING THE LIES

We are all tempted to believe lies from the villain. What are the lies you're hearing over and over? Keep a running list of the lies you're being fed over the course of a day. Maybe it's that you're not enough or that there's no way God *really* loves you. Be as honest with yourself as you can.

Next, counter those lies with the truth of Scripture. Remember: The only way to defeat a lie is with the truth.

CHAPTER 7

THE VILLAIN DISUNIFIES

REMEMBER AT THE BEGINNING OF THE BOOK when we flashed back to 2020 and the chaos that ensued that year? A few months before, at the end of 2019, I sensed God was telling me that 2020 was going to be a difficult year. I was not quite sure what that meant or why, but as I was trying to listen and hear from God, that's what I was hearing.

In early January, an issue popped up at church that came and went pretty quickly. *Whew!* I thought. Maybe it wasn't going to be such a difficult year after all. Maybe I misheard something. However, what unfolded over the next few months was the greatest leadership challenge I have ever faced.

In early 2020, we were bombarded with new confirmed cases of COVID-19 and images of hospitals being overrun with patients. I remember where I was when the NBA shut down. The NBA! They called off the season right before games tipped off, with arenas full of fans waiting. Then, state by state, new guidelines were being issued.

Our staff held meeting after meeting, trying to figure out how to best care for people we may not be able to see in person. Toilet paper became a valuable commodity. Within our staff, people held varying convictions. In our church, people held varying convictions. Some people thought we were reckless and unsafe, while others thought we were overreacting and fearing an illness that they thought had been blown out of proportion.

We saw disunity in families over where each person's convictions landed. There were arguments in small groups. Different cities, states, and the entire country seemed to be on different pages. A few months later, on top of the pandemic, we saw escalated tension over the racial divide in our land. To add to the conflict, this was all happening during an election year. Divide, divide, divide. That was the plan all along.

Honestly, Satan's plan worked. I have never felt more conflict in my life. I have never seen more division in my lifetime. People I love, care about, and respect ended up divided as a result of the chaos of 2020. I saw angst and frustration and bitterness bubble over. And it makes sense to me that it would all start with a meeting in the dark realm.

THE AFTERMATH

In some ways, it will take decades for us to fully understand the fallout from 2020. Social scientists are working as fast as they can to wrap their minds around the paradigm shifts right now. In 2022, the World Health Organization reported a rise in anxiety and depression of 25 percent globally since the pandemic began.[1]

A Pew Research study in 2021 reported that 88 percent of US respondents agreed that the country was *more* divided than before the pandemic began.[2] Young people, in particular, were impacted. In a study of 7,700 high school students in 2021, the Centers for Disease Control found that 40 percent of teenagers said they persistently felt sad or hopeless during the previous year, and among the 43 percent of students who consumed alcohol, 30 percent of those said their drinking levels rose during the pandemic.[3]

Isolation went up. Suicide rates went up. Political polarization went up. Divide, divide, divide. Anecdotally, I could tell you hundreds of stories of how I watched this play out over the course of a couple of years. As I would talk to pastor friends around the country, they were seeing it too. The ability to get rational, Jesus-professing people in the room, at a table, across from one another, to sort out their differences seemed to vanish, almost overnight.

Instead, people isolated. They pulled away. Their churches became less and less of a priority and that person, that pastor, that fellow small group member who believed differently or had different convictions than them was now an enemy. Their allegiance shifted from Jesus to their favorite news network and how willing they were to go along with (or defy) stay-at-home orders. And I am convinced it was all a work of the Enemy.

THAT TIME JESUS PRAYED FOR US

Part of the villain's playbook has always been division and disunity. Think back to the garden of Eden in Genesis 3. Not only did he drive a wedge between God and humanity when Eve took that first bite of fruit, but he also divided the very first husband and wife. Their offspring? One son killed another during a fit of rage. The pattern continued all throughout the Old Testament.

Division between God and His people and division among the people themselves. Wherever there is even the slightest crack of division, the Enemy hopes to turn it into a canyon.

By the time Jesus arrived on the earth, He knew full well that division was one of the Enemy's tactics to try and stop the momentum of the movement happening around Him. Jesus' solution? Prayer.

Were you aware that Jesus prayed for you when He was here on this earth? It is well documented. What did He pray? Did He pray, "I pray that their kids would be successful in athletics and that they would all make good grades, and I pray that they would have a white picket fence and a German shepherd and as many children as their hearts desire"?

No. Thankfully, Jesus' moment of prayer for you has been documented and preserved by the Holy Spirit. You can read it today. Jesus was about to be arrested, beaten, and ultimately crucified. He was talking to the Father, pleading with God. What did He ask for His children? Let's see what John 17:20–23 says.

> "I pray also for those who will believe in me through their message, *that all of them may be one*, Father, just as you are in me and I am in you. May they also be in us so that the world may believe that you have sent me. I have given them the glory that you gave me, that they may be one as we are one—I in them and you in me—so that they may be brought to complete unity. Then the world will know that you sent me and have loved them even as you have loved me." (emphasis added)

When Jesus was here, Jesus prayed to the Father for you that Christians—His followers, who live alongside one another in this assembly we know as church—would get along and live in unity. But why that? Of all the things Jesus could have prayed for, why not protection from suffering or enough money that we don't have to sweat it out paycheck to paycheck? It's because when you and I live in unity, the world sees something different from what they experience anywhere else other than the church.

WHY DOES IT MATTER?

Have you ever wondered why unity is important? Who cares if we are unified? Why do we need to be unified? Why can we not just be individualistic and lone-wolf our faith until Jesus calls us home? Why can we not go about it in our own ways? Why should we not just continue to watch our favorite pastor from home in our pajamas with a cup of coffee? Why is it even important that we get along?

Unity is an apologetic—a defense of our faith—to a world that is so easily divided. So if the world sees Christians whose bond in Jesus overrides politics and preferences, they say, "That Jesus guy must have been real. He must have come from the Father. There is no other reason those people would get along." I believe that message has been lost somewhere along the way, so that's why I want you to know explicitly that this is what Jesus prayed for you.

Do you realize that, by being a part of a Bible-teaching, healthy church, you have a bigger target on your back? If your church is dysfunctional and nobody gets along and everyone has their own agenda, that is playing right into the villain's hand. Satan is always after works of God. For some people, that freaks them out. They hear that and they want out, because they didn't mean to sign up for that. They're thinking, *Man, I don't want to be under attack. I don't want the Enemy to know who I am.*

The alternative way is living a faithless life, full of indulging in your own pleasure. He will leave you alone and will not want anything to do with you. You will be benign for the kingdom of God. But if you start walking in faith and pushing back darkness, you'd better believe the Enemy is going to attack you by every means possible as you journey home.

It's no secret that churches are dying everywhere. Longtime, established churches dwindle and eventually close their doors. What is happening to us? A few years ago, I read an article in *The Atlantic* about the decline in faith in the United States.[4] The article discussed "America's epidemic of empty churches." It talked about how, all throughout America, churches are closing and being turned into skate parks, civic centers, community centers, gathering places, and coworking spaces. What happened to those churches? Why would a church ever close?

Can I tell you what happened? From the outside, it seems like a simple economics problem. A few members left, then they couldn't pay their mortgage, so they had to shut it down. To the church members, more often than not, the reason is different: a force comes in from the outside, and they turn on each other. They don't get along. Their focus fades. They crumble from the inside out. It happens over and over.

Churches have split and divided over dozens of issues. A couple of decades ago, church after church imploded over arguments that started over the style (and volume) of the music. The Enemy found an issue and drove a wedge between people over a matter of preference. Then it was Sunday school versus small groups, or the pastor wearing jeans or a suit. Or fill-in-the-blank with any other issues that started off seemingly small and ultimately divided people. As you try to figure out where these churches' problems started, the explanations themselves sound ridiculous. Unless there is something more going on.

APPRECIATING THE DIFFERENCES

In his book *The Jesus Way*, pastor and author Eugene Peterson wrote, "The devil does some of his best work behind stained glass."[5] In a place where there should be unity and a spirit of peace, the Enemy works even harder to sow discord and disunity. Why is it easy? Because inside the church there are dozens, hundreds, or thousands of uniquely created people made in the image of God with their own stories, backgrounds, wirings, and differences. When we lose sight of that, the Enemy is winning.

Almost twenty years ago, Monica and I were new believers. We had heard our church talk a lot about small groups and how we should be in one, so, trying to do the right thing, we joined one. I walked into a living room and I met four guys I had never met before. Three of them were engineers. They had all graduated from Texas A&M, and they seemed to be clones of the same person. Two of them drove a white '92 Camry. I didn't know if you just get that when you graduate from A&M or what. I remember thinking, *This is so confusing.* I had nothing in common with them. I had pulled up in a Jaguar and a pinstripe suit, eager to meet new friends. Man, was I disappointed.

When Monica and I got in the car at the end of the night, I looked at her and said, "Well, we are never going back to that." That kept on for a good five years. Really—for five years I did not like those guys, nor did I enjoy going. But we kept going back. Everything in me wanted to cut and run with that group. Living alongside other believers in close community is never easy. Fourteen years later, as we moved from Dallas to Waco (along with one of those couples I did not like back then), those people were closer than my best friends. Leaving them was gut-wrenching. We had laughed together, cried together, celebrated together, and endured every high and low of the previous fourteen years together. They were family.

When we joined a small group in Waco, we started to build that up again. Then we went through a season when we dealt with what seemed like a never-resolved conflict. Every week it felt like it compounded itself. Finally, it was like a lightbulb went off as I looked across the living room and said, "I think somewhere along the way we stopped appreciating each other's differences." We stopped believing the best about one another. And the Enemy loved it.

The New Testament uses a metaphor when describing the way the church interacts: a body. Different parts, same body. The problem is, the hands often don't like how the feet can't hold on to things. And the feet feel proud that they can easily balance the whole body on themselves. Typically in church settings, you're wired one way, and someone else in the body has different wiring. And because your wirings and your giftings from the Holy Spirit (your God-given gifts) are different, you naturally handle situations differently. But when you think you are right and they are wrong, you begin to resent each other.

Say someone has the gifts of mercy and compassion—they feel deep empathy. And someone else has a gift of exhortation, truth telling, teaching, and/or prophecy. Those two people will handle situations completely differently. They might begin to resent each other. One person says, "You are enabling them. Stop enabling." The other person says, "Wow. You are so harsh. Why would you be unkind?" In reality, they are both operating within their spiritual gifts.

All kinds of people make up the body of Christ. We can appreciate different people's giftings without resenting them. There is a person who coddles and cries and cares for and shows mercy. Then there is a person who is courageous and speaks truth. The person who coddles also has to learn to share truth. The person who is courageous also must learn to be kind. The only way we can learn that is from each other.

God is in the process—by the power of His Holy Spirit—of conforming us to the image and the character of His Son. And He uses other believers around us to do this. Some of us cannot stand somebody wired differently than us. We need to beg God for more grace, a softer heart, that we would be able to lock arms and be the most powerful force the world has ever seen. In our diversity, we can experience unity under the one love of Jesus Christ. That is when the world is confused. That's when they say, "What's going on over there?" But what typically happens is all the mercy people group together and go to one church. They say, "No, we can't stand those prophetic truth people. Let's meet up over here and love people." It's like the body trying to walk on its hands. It's clumsy.

Then you get the prophets, exhorters, and admonishers. They all group together. If they started a business, it would be successful because they are driven and go without sleep. They say, "Let's go!" Then they all meet and plant a church. And they will kick you in the face with their hard-charging doctrine. It would be a total beating in the long term.

The real church—a healthy church—is made up of all the giftings. In it, you'll see an appreciation for one another. The prophet can look across the living room and say, "I love the way you love people." The merciful person can say, "I love the way you boldly share truth." Everybody can use their gifts together. That's what it means to pursue unity in our diversity.

TAKING US OFF MISSION

Toward the end of his letter to the church in Philippi, the apostle Paul called out two members of the church who were in conflict.

It was affecting the rest of the church. There was some issue causing disunity among them, therefore halting the momentum of the
church. Paul said this as he started to wrap up the letter:

> I plead with Euodia and I plead with Syntyche to be of the same
> mind in the Lord. Yes, and I ask you, my true companion, help
> these women since they have contended at my side in the cause
> of the gospel, along with Clement and the rest of my co-workers,
> whose names are in the book of life. (Philippians 4:2–3)

We don't know a lot about these women. This is the only mention of them in all of antiquity (which is honestly a bummer for
them—I bet they had redemptive qualities too). They were divided
and disagreed on their opinions on something, and word had
traveled all the way back to Paul. Paul cared enough about unity
within the Philippian church to mention this and to address them
by name.

Why? The mission of God was at stake. Any time a conflict
pops up between believers, their focus goes off the mission and
the Enemy gains ground. Sometimes we can get into fruitless
arguments because we are not focused enough on the gospel. The
gospel is not a big enough priority to us. The gospel, though it is
simple, is also complex. We continue to surrender our lives to it
daily, and we should move forward in our understanding of it,
which leads to our growth in maturity.

Disunity in the church is almost always a sign of immaturity.
Somewhere in disunity there is usually someone given to pride,
wanting to win, wanting their preferences to win out, or not taking the time and patience to see an alternative perspective from
the other side. When we're in it to win, it causes a wedge between
us and other believers. The longer the conflict lasts, the larger that
divide becomes.

I shared earlier and I will share it again: Most church splits are the work of Satan. Not all of them, but most of them. The work of the Enemy combines with this issue of immaturity to produce destruction. That is why Paul was pleading with the two women (along with everyone else in the church) to move toward restoration. Unresolved conflict is a distraction and stands in the way of the gospel advancing.

If you want to keep the Enemy from causing disunity among the believers around you, it's going to take a lot of time. It takes a lot of effort and courage, it is often exhausting, and you will hardly ever feel like doing it. People say all the time to me that they are just not quite ready to resolve their issues.

Spoiler: You are not ever going to feel ready. The goal is not to feel ready, but to run toward the problem instead of running away. Fighting for unity is a step toward fighting the Enemy.

MAKE IT STICK: PRACTICING RECONCILIATION

The Enemy loves when we live in conflict with other believers. For many of us, the hardest part is admitting that we own part of the conflict (no matter how large or how small our part is).

Ask God to bring to mind any believers you are not currently fully reconciled to. What harm did you do to them? Even if they don't seek forgiveness and reconciliation from you, what part of the conflict could you take ownership of? Reach out to them this week and seek reconciliation so the gospel can continue to move forward and is no longer hindered by conflict.

CHAPTER 8

THE VILLAIN DESENSITIZES

NOT LONG AFTER MONICA AND I GOT MARRIED WE made the drive down from Dallas to visit some friends from college who were living in Houston. As we turned into their neighborhood, I saw all our friends out in the street playing a game of touch football. I threw the car into park, ran over to the huddle, and said, "I'm in!" I sized up the friend who was guarding me and told the quarterback to throw me a post route. I had a few inches on the guy (to go along with my 4.9 blazing speed), so this would be easy.

He tossed it up to me and I, in an amazing display of athleticism, leaped up to catch the ball. Somehow my body did a flip in the air, causing me to land on my head. My first memory was waking up to everybody huddled around me asking if I was okay. We had been there all of thirty-seven seconds and suddenly this visit wasn't going at all how we had planned. After a car ride to the hospital consisting of friends asking me the same five questions over and over, a doctor confirmed that it was a concussion and I should be back to normal soon.

The next morning I woke up feeling better, so I made my way to the coffee pot. I poured a cup and spat it out instantly. It tasted terrible! Everyone else seemed to think it tasted fine, but it was the worst coffee I'd ever had. Then I sat down to eat a chocolate bar for breakfast (don't judge) and it tasted terrible too. Had it gone bad? Can chocolate bars even do that? Then the weirdest thing of all happened: We were all loaded up in the car driving to dinner, and we passed a skunk on the side of the road. Everybody started talking about the terrible smell, but I had no idea what they were talking about. I thought it smelled like potpourri!

That one fall onto the concrete had done something to my brain. All my senses had gone completely out of whack. The things I'd grown to love tasted terrible and repulsed me. The things that should have repulsed me were suddenly a breath of fresh air. While the desensitization came and went very quickly, it was definitely an unnerving experience.

UNDERSTANDING DESENSITIZATION

If you have ever experienced a sudden change in your physical senses, you know that it's a disorienting feeling. Spiritually speaking, the Enemy uses desensitization against us every day, but it is far more gradual. Over time, we become desensitized to sin and the effects it has on us. One of the greatest tactics the Enemy uses against us is the ability to make us numb to the effects and consequences of our sin.

When we are submitted to the Spirit of God and we are walking closely with Jesus, fully devoted to Him, and living in obedience to His command, we *should* feel the effects of our sin. We should feel conviction, a desire to repent and turn away from that sin. But the more normalized and habitual the sin is, the less we feel the weight of it. Suddenly, it can become that thing we do or, even worse, who we are.

Psychologists have been interested in the concept of desensitization for a while. The premise is quite simple: The more we consume of something, the more used to it our brains (or bodies) become. From a young age, we are formed by what we consume, and this continues on into adulthood. For example, as early as the 1950s people started showing concern that violence depicted in media was leading to more aggressive behaviors in children and adolescents.

In 2009, the American Academy of Pediatrics even published a study warning of the potential long-term consequences of consuming violent media.[1] Why? Because they were concerned about the desensitization of an entire generation.

As Christians, we don't think about this Enemy tactic nearly enough. It is a crafty tool, and it affects us over a long period of time. As you read through the New Testament, particularly Paul's letters, you can see all the warning signs of desensitization. We've talked about the tactic of destruction—those momentous, at times life-altering moments like Job experienced. We have also talked about distraction, and the Enemy doing his very best to take our eye off the ball long enough to take us off mission. If we're really pursuing Jesus for the long haul, we're going to have ample opportunities to be knocked off course. Sometimes these will feel like catastrophic moments. Other times it happens more subtly.

Desensitization is different because the villain is slow-playing us, trying to numb us to how harmful sin actually is. Even worse, the villain can try to convince us that sin is not even sin at all.

REDIRECTING YOUR WORLDVIEW

In 2023, a movie called *Nefarious* came out. If you have made it this far into this book, you would likely be interested in the movie as well. It tells the story of a man on death row who claims to be possessed by a demon named Nefarious. The movie has been likened to a modern-day film adaptation of *The Screwtape Letters* by C. S. Lewis. Most of the movie takes place with two men seated across the table from one another as James, a government-hired psychiatrist, is trying to determine whether this man claiming to be possessed by a demon is fit to face execution.

At one point in the movie, Nefarious begins talking about how modern culture has deteriorated to the point that people are unaware of how wicked it actually is. He says:

> We achieved our goal. Slowly. With your movies, your TV, and your media. We desensitized you. Redirected your worldview. To the point that you can't recognize evil when it's right in front of your face. More to the point, James, you can't even feel it when you're doing it.[2]

abortion pornography alcohol etc

Slowly but surely, we come under the influence of something (or someone) other than God. It creeps in, it seems harmless at first, then it becomes normalized. Look back at every cultural shift we have seen that moved us away from the heart of God over the past century. These things did not happen overnight. Rather, they came one day at a time. The point this movie is making is similar to the one the apostle Paul made in his letter to the church in Ephesus. Toward the end of the letter, Paul wrote:

Wow That's our society

movies media entertainment

> So I tell you this, and insist on it in the Lord, that you must no longer live as the Gentiles do, in the futility of their thinking. They are darkened in their understanding and separated from the life of God because of the ignorance that is in them due to the hardening of their hearts. Having lost all sensitivity, they have given themselves over to sensuality so as to indulge

in every kind of impurity, and they are full of greed. That, however, is not the way of life you learned when you heard about
Christ and were taught in him in accordance with the truth that
is in Jesus. (Ephesians 4:17–21)

Paul's point here is simple: If you have placed your faith in
Jesus, you can't live as the pagans do. Their hearts hardened, and
they lost all sensitivity to what was of God and what was not,
so they gave themselves over to their passions and indulged in
whatever felt good or right in the moment. They lived greedy,
indulgent, impure lives. If you look around today, the same could
be said of our culture. The goal is to accumulate the most stuff
and money and to live a hedonistic life for our seventy-seven-ish
years on earth. But notice that last verse: It's calling us back to a
life consistent with the way that Jesus taught us to live.

Each week after the Sunday service, I stand in front of the
stage and meet with anyone who wants to talk. People are pro-
cessing what they just heard in the message, and it is always a
great time to help them work through how to apply what they
just learned to whatever situation is going on in their lives. One
Sunday, a young woman stood off to the side, clearly wanting to
talk but not sure where to begin. As the line thinned out, she came
forward and cut right to the chase.

"I need your help," she said. "I only date losers, and I don't
know what is wrong with me."

I appreciated her candor. I responded, "Let me ask you a couple
of questions. Who is your favorite musical artist? What are you
listening to as you drive around town?" A little taken aback, she
said Taylor Swift and Drake, but she likes a lot of different artists.

Next, I asked her what her favorite TV show was. At that
point, she reminded me of her original problem and again wanted
to know why she only dated losers. I asked again what her favorite

show was. *The Bachelor*, she responded. She told me she was unsure how any of this related back to the problem at hand.

I told her it had *everything* to do with her problem. She was conditioning her mind to the point where her worldview was misaligned with what a biblical worldview looked like. As she drove around town listening to songs about unhealthy relationships and then flipped on her favorite show, which is also centered around unhealthy relationships, it seemed obvious why she found herself in a pattern of unhealthy relationships.

WHAT YOU FEED GROWS

The villain is so crafty. He takes a message he wants to saturate our minds with, puts a slick beat behind it or a compelling storyline alongside it, and we cannot wait to consume it. It leaves us with a distorted worldview, all while wanting more in the process.

Paul was talking about a similar situation throughout several of his letters in the New Testament. In Philippians 3:18–19, he said:

> As I have often told you before and now tell you again even with tears, many live as enemies of the cross of Christ. Their destiny is destruction, their god is their stomach, and their glory is in their shame. Their mind is set on earthly things.

Now, to make this really clear: Paul was talking about sin. He was talking about our sinful desires, our sinful appetites. Some people see this world as their buffet line, and they eat whatever they want. They follow every desire. Their appetite is their god, and their glory is their shame. They boast about an indulgence in the things Jesus died for.

We know that the more you eat, the more your appetite grows.

This is one of the lessons in ministry that I have seen on full display over and over: Whatever you feed grows. If I am thinking anxious thoughts and I feel trapped by fear, and then I go scroll through the news app on my phone or watch an hour of cable news, I am feeding the problem. I am perpetuating the cycle. What I am feeding is growing out of control.

Often I talk with college students and young adults who are living out my past story. They are drinking to excess. Smoking weed. When that's not enough, they keep experimenting with new drugs, looking for new highs. When those get dull, they turn to something else. Then something else. Then something else. When you live this way, it sears your conscience (1 Timothy 4:1–2). Right and wrong goes away and every weekday is just one day closer to the weekend when you do it all over again.

I had felt the need to indulge all these vices in my life. I kept upping the ante and finding new habits and sin patterns to fall into. My addictions grew further and further out of my control until the Holy Spirit started to do a new work in my heart. In his book *Counterfeit Gods*, pastor Tim Keller wrote, "An idolatrous attachment can lead you to break any promise, rationalize any indiscretion, or betray any other allegiance, in order to hold on to it. It may drive you to violate all good and proper boundaries. To practice idolatry is to be a slave."[3]

When I say "whatever you feed grows," I'm talking about being enslaved to whatever it is that you are feeding. And once you realize it, it can take a long time to break those cycles. The Enemy will continue putting opportunities to sin in front of us, one thing leading to another leading to another . . . and we become numb to all of it. We don't think about what it does to our relationship with our Creator. We don't think about the impact it has on others. We can get selfish and indulgent, and sometimes we don't even realize it.

THE SOLOMON EXPERIMENT

One of the most interesting figures in the Old Testament is King Solomon. If you are unaware, he was the son of King David. After David died, Solomon assumed the throne. When God told Solomon that He would give him whatever he asked for, Solomon didn't ask for more money, more power, or more land. Instead, he asked God for wisdom. God granted him that but also gave him more wealth than we could even comprehend. All of a sudden, he became the wisest and wealthiest man to ever live.

Solomon had every material possession you could ever want. He had more money than he knew what to do with. He was the single most powerful person alive on the planet during his reign. And he was the wisest man alive! If you are anything like me, you read about his life and it seems like he would have nothing to complain about. What else could the guy want?

This is the guy who seemingly had it all. But even Solomon was trying to find the meaning of life. The book of Ecclesiastes is part his autobiography, part lament, and part a cautionary tale. He found that his wealth was fleeting. His pursuit of earthly pleasure led him to having seven hundred wives and three hundred concubines. Ecclesiastes is Solomon telling the story of his life and the lessons that he learned along the way. What did he find? Solomon had discovered that life "under the sun"—a phrase he used nearly thirty times to describe life on this earth—is meaningless. He had searched everywhere. He had experienced pleasure. He had spent the money. He had accumulated the power. All of it had left him feeling empty.

But how? Why? It seems that the very thing Solomon had is what many of us—Christians and non-Christians alike—devote our lives to chasing. Solomon looked around toward the end of his life with a profound feeling of emptiness. There are only so many highs you can chase and so many conquests you can achieve before feelings fade and numbness sets in. The Enemy wants you to keep chasing and chasing.   Yep

Once I became a Christian, I would try explaining what my life looked like before Christ to people who didn't know me before. I would always say, "I was everything wrong with Dallas in a person." Now, if you have never lived in Dallas (or spent much time there), I know that example falls a little flat. But I was materialistic, I was chasing girls, I was part of the club scene. I cared about fancy cars and nice suits. I cared about ascending the corporate ladder. I was unaware of it at the time, but I was trying to be my own (much lesser) version of Solomon.

Looking back at that season of my life, with twenty-twenty hindsight, I can see just how empty it all was. I had given in to every temptation the Enemy put in front of me, and there was no such thing as excess in my life. After walking alongside people in vocational ministry for the past fifteen-plus years, I see the same emptiness in the eyes of others I meet. By every worldly standard, they "have it all," but I can see the emptiness caused by their own sin. Something that usually starts off small spirals out of control, and it usually begins with the small compromises.

DO NOT GIVE THE DEVIL
A FOOTHOLD

In pastoral ministry, I've walked alongside a number of people and families in crisis. As I said earlier, so much of ministry is pattern recognition. One thing I have learned over the years is that very, very, very seldom (I hesitate to say "never") does someone wreck their life overnight. Very rarely do people wake up one morning and say, "Today is the day I want to throw it all away." They get there gradually as one pet sin turns into another pet sin, which then turns into even more sin.

In Ephesians 4:27, Paul said that we are not to give the devil even a foothold. Every time you sin, you are cracking the door open for the Enemy to come in. When you follow that hashtag, go to that website, say those words, hang out with those people, drink that stuff, smoke that thing—whatever your thing is—when you cross that line of what is holy and God-honoring, you crack the door and invite the Enemy into your life. Each time you give in to temptation, the door opens wider and wider, making it that much harder to kick the Enemy back out. This is *key* to understanding spiritual warfare. When you sin, you let him in.

Every year our family attends a summer camp, and this camp has a climbing wall, the kind you've likely seen before. You get harnessed to a rope and someone either spots you or hooks you up to an automatic pulley system that supports you as you try to climb one foothold and handhold after the other. I am a big guy, so it's always challenging for me because of my weight, but I watch these kids go straight up the wall one hand and one foot after the other. All they have to hold on to is a little piece of polycarbonate that protrudes from the wall, barely big enough to hold their grips. Their toes cling to the piece beneath them.

Every choice that you make not to trust God (otherwise known as sin) is a foothold or handhold for the Enemy that leaves you more susceptible to attack. This is why Scripture says to not give the devil even a foothold. It is such a powerful image to help the passage come alive, because every time you choose to sin, you are inviting him into your life, to partner with him. If you let him in, now he has a grip, and as you sin again, he begins to climb. The Enemy begins to climb farther, and as you continue in the path of sin, he devours your life. He controls your life, and the only solution you have is repentance—to turn away from your sin and toward Jesus.

I once walked alongside a guy who had confessed to an affair. In one of our conversations, we tried to trace everything that had happened to where it began. If you're anything like me, you would assume that it started with some kind of hidden sexual addiction or a serial struggle with pornography. This was different, though. I will never forget what he said one night. He told me, "I have always rolled through stop signs." At first, I sat there confused. I asked him to connect the dots for me because I thought he was speaking metaphorically. As he talked through his life up until that point, he'd always been casual about authority and rules.

As you read that, you may think, *What's the big deal? I rolled through a stop sign yesterday, and I'm fine.* And I believe that's the point. Those seemingly small compromises of integrity—the things we do when no one else is looking or paying attention—may not seem like a big deal, but they can easily kick-start an avalanche of choices that lead to the Enemy taking us out. He'll leave us enslaved to sin and impotent as a disciple-maker in the kingdom of God. Every time we justify a compromise and crack the door open for the Enemy, we are being desensitized without even realizing it.

Toward the beginning of his letter to the church in Rome, Paul wrote of a religious culture that was a little like ours today. He was longing to go visit Rome because he had heard of all the ways the people who had heard the gospel, who knew how to live, were no longer doing what they knew to be right. He went on to say this:

> They have become filled with every kind of wickedness, evil, greed and depravity. They are full of envy, murder, strife, deceit and malice. They are gossips, slanderers, God-haters, insolent, arrogant and boastful; they invent ways of doing evil; they disobey their parents; they have no understanding, no fidelity, no love, no mercy. Although they know God's righteous decree

our current culture

that those who do such things deserve death, they not only continue to do these very things but also approve of those who practice them. (Romans 1:29–32)

What Paul was describing here—particularly in that final sentence—is a culture that has grown numb to sin and wickedness. They knew what was right. They knew what was wrong. But they had not only opted to continue living in sin, they'd also given an approving nod to those around them living in the same manner. When we get to the point where those who know better live and approve of sin, the Enemy can check those believers off as impotent and move on to the next target.

✗ parents who were raised in the church now approving of their child's gender confusion lifestyle

In the next section, we'll talk more about how to fight back against the Enemy, but as we consider this warning to not give the devil a foothold, keep an eye out for where you may be experiencing desensitization.

MAKE IT STICK: AUDIT THE FOOTHOLDS

To understand where you've been desensitized, you will need to set aside time for introspection and invite in accountability. Think through the following questions. Then ask trusted friends in the faith to serve as a mirror into your life, and tell you where they see any desensitization in you. Be fully transparent with them. Tell them everything they need to know to best walk alongside you. Ask the Spirit to help you walk in humility as they speak into your life.

Ask yourself:

Where have I given the Enemy a foothold in my life?
Where do I have the door cracked open, even if just slightly?

— Where am I inviting the Enemy to desensitize me to the gravity of my sin?

Write down your answers. Text them to your small group and ask for help and for prayer. Tell your pastor. You need to be hyperaware of the answers to these questions because that's where you will be most susceptible to the attacks of the Enemy.

CHAPTER 9

THE VILLAIN DECONSTRUCTS

ONCE UPON A TIME, I TOOK A REAL ESTATE INVEST-ment course so I could flip houses. Keep in mind, I am not a contractor. I am not the guy you're going to call to build something for you. But I do love houses—new, old, traditional, modern—and I enjoy the design process, so it felt like a fun way to make some extra money doing something I enjoyed. And it was—but it was also a *ton* of work. I have horror stories of all that can go wrong in the house renovation process. Rats, black mold, gas leaks, foundation issues . . . I've seen it all. And that list was actually from one house!

When Chip and Joanna Gaines started filming episodes of *Fixer Upper* around 2014, the nation quickly took notice. It became the number one show on HGTV and landed the Gaines family on billboards and *The Tonight Show,* and it helped highlight the city of Waco in a positive light. The premise of the show is simple: Find the cheapest house in a great neighborhood, knock down some walls, freshen it up with some paint and new windows, and at the end of an hour a family has a beautiful home of their own for a fraction of the cost of building a brand-new house. And they could do it all in one hour, including commercials!

In every episode, the first thing that would happen once the house was purchased would be "demo day." Everything not staying in the house had to go. A small army of guys with sledgehammers would head to the house and start taking down walls, knocking out drywall, and ripping out the cabinets that needed to go. On the show, this consisted of a few cut scenes set to music that would last a few minutes. They made it look easy. But it is hard work. Necessary, but hard. To rebuild the house, demo day had to happen. To build the new walls and install the new appliances, there had to be a lot of tearing down.

Deconstruction is a real buzzword in Christianity today. I have had conversations many times with countless people, in person and online, who are at some point in their own deconstruction journey. What started off as a word to describe "I have some questions about faith" has evolved over the past few years to mean something a little bit different to everyone. This happens with language all the time, but as time goes on the word gets twisted and becomes this blanket term that gets tossed around too much. Like many other matters of faith, it is nuanced and complicated.

Questions are not a negative thing—God can handle all your questions, doubts, and wrestling. And more than that, questioning God isn't a new phenomenon. The book of Psalms, in particular, is full of raw, honest, questioning prayers. But I believe there is a healthy and unhealthy way to engage in this process.

NEW WORD, OLD TACTIC

The more I have thought about it, the more I'm convinced deconstruction has become a new word for an old tactic of the Enemy trying to separate people from God. It comes in many different forms and can look a thousand different ways for a thousand different people, but at the end of the day, the Enemy simply wants you to walk away from your faith. If he can make you question the goodness of God, he can move you off mission and over to the sidelines where you will be less effective for the kingdom of God. He wants to put a wedge between you and God.

As I pastor people and walk alongside them through seasons of doubt, I have seen that most questions can be put into five categories:

- Is God real?
- Is God powerful?
- Is God good?
- Is God for me?
- Can I trust God's people (i.e., the church)?

When I meet people struggling in their faith, most of the time they are questioning one of those five things. The Enemy has come in with a flaming arrow and has caused them to doubt one (or all) of those truths.

If you think back to the garden of Eden in Genesis 3, the Enemy used deception (which we have already covered), but we also see the first deconstruction in Scripture. The serpent's use of "Did God really say that?" was the first of many attempts in recorded history to get people to doubt what God says. It's still happening today. When Christians encounter passages in the Bible that are confusing, countercultural, or contrary to what we are comfortable with, many of us start asking the same question: Did God *really* say that? And we answer, *Surely that means something else. Surely God never said that.*

Sometimes faith gets tough. You look up one day and you are

hit with some real challenges and hardships. Maybe it is something at work, relationships, church, finances—just the normal life stuff that comes up—and you start to wrestle more and ask, "Am I sure about this Jesus guy?" That's when you begin to reconsider all things. The next step is the question, "Am I sure I am in the correct lane of Christianity?" Sometimes that is cloaked in, "Is there something out there closer to the truth?" But really, so many people are asking, "Is there something out there less hard?"

I see person after person go on this deconstruction journey of reading or watching or listening to some rogue theologian on a podcast trying to find some tributary idea that might be a simpler form of Christianity, rather than the orthodox fairway that has survived in the church for thousands of years. They often want something that will allow them to continue in a bad habit or relationship. They want a faith that doesn't call them to say hard things to people they love. They often see a problem in the world and make God the scapegoat or they need to make sense of something they've experienced. And I get it—I have walked this road myself.

MY OWN JOURNEY

In my early years, I went through a season of doubt before placing my faith in Jesus. Deconstruction for me looked like erasing the whiteboard of everything I had been taught. As I have shared, I grew up Catholic and went to Catholic school. My dad was Catholic, my mom was Lutheran, and then I went to the Baptist youth group because that was where the cutest girls were. By the time I was eighteen and not walking with the Lord (which is quite an understatement), I'd had a lot of different church experiences.

As I got older, I started thinking about all the different religions out there. What about Islam? What about Judaism? After all, had I been born in India there is a strong likelihood I would have been born into a Hindu family. I had way more questions than answers in that season, but I kept on searching. For a while, when it came to faith, it felt like I was in a loop of perpetual demo days. I was the guy with the sledgehammer, knocking down wall after wall. And I was not ready to rebuild anything in its place yet; I just needed to keep knocking down walls in hopes of finding answers. God is not afraid of our difficult questions. God knows His truth will always prevail if we seek it. The villain, however, loves it when we don't seek answers. He loves to leave us confused.

In hindsight, I find it interesting that I kept tripping over the person of Jesus. There was something so compelling to me about how this one man reset the calendar (today's year is the number of years from his birth) and started a movement that continues to this day. Jesus stayed at the foundation of it all for me. As many walls as I knocked down and rebuilt, I did not tear apart the foundation because I could not get past the person of Jesus. Once I placed my faith in Jesus in my early twenties, I knew I could at least bank on Jesus.

So, I just walked up to the dry-erase board and tried to mentally erase everything else I knew. I said, "All right, I just want to start from scratch. I want to understand who God is straight from the source." I erased it and began to build and think, *Okay, what is true?* If I were on a deserted island and nobody else had ever told me who God is and I just started reading the Bible, what would I believe about God? If the Holy Spirit chose to preserve the sixty-six books in the Bible, written over thousands of years, and placed it in my hand to teach me everything I need to know about God illuminated by the Holy Spirit, what would I want to know? What would I need to know? And that's how you start rebuilding your theology. Reconstructing. You need the source of truth.

In the early phases of my reconstruction journey, I decided

I could trust the Bible. I had to answer that question because, during the deconstruction phase, people were saying things like, "Well, you know it has been changed throughout the years. In the Dark Ages there were words that were wiped out. Entire books are missing. What about the book of Enoch? What about the Gospel of Thomas?" I got busy reading credible sources and researching the hundreds of hours of work that other scholars had done. Once I actually searched out the answers to my questions, the evidence was overwhelming that the Bible could be trusted. We have more manuscripts than ever. The Scripture gets more reliable the more ancient manuscripts we find. They match up. They tell the same story. Once I concluded the Bible could be trusted as God's Word, I started relearning and reforming my theology for myself. I had to relearn who God is and what He desires from me, and, all these years later, I am still in that relearning process.

If you think about it, Christianity started with the Jews deconstructing (and then reconstructing). They had their way of doing things for thousands of years. God had made covenants with His people, He asked them to follow the Law, and for centuries they tried their best (all while failing at the same time) to uphold their end of the bargain. And all the while, there was a long-standing promise that a Messiah was going to come and right all that was wrong in the world.

Jesus showed up and started inviting these grown men to come follow Him and learn from Him. They called him "Rabbi," which is the Hebrew word for "teacher." This teacher—Jesus—did things differently. He started talking about a whole new kingdom He was building. After His resurrection, He left behind disciples who started by taking Jewish traditions and rebuilding Christianity on top of them. One example of this is Peter and John going to the temple to worship (on a Saturday!) in Acts 3. Why did they do that? It was their custom; it was what they had always done.

I am so passionate about this topic: You must build on the death and the resurrection of Jesus Christ for the forgiveness of your sins. When someone says, "I don't know what I believe anymore," my answer is always the same. I say, "Tell me, what do you believe about Jesus? Let's start there. Who is He?" We can get to the age of the earth later. We can get to dinosaurs. We can get to secondary and tertiary theological topics. Tell me what you believe about Jesus. The reason the disciples were able to reconstruct, after all they had been through, is that they had encountered Jesus. They had a whole new cornerstone to rebuild on top of.

WALKING ALONGSIDE OTHERS

I have walked alongside countless people in ministry, including several close friends, as they process through what they believe. We can label this process different things—"crisis of faith," "season of doubt," "wrestling with God," "deconstruction"—but generally it's all the same idea. They usually experience some kind of incident (maybe even one like in the other chapters we have covered in this book) that brings them to a place of wondering, *What do I actually believe?* From there, this process can go one of many ways.

Some go into "throw it all out" mode. My heart always moves toward this person because the Enemy sees them as susceptible and wants to put up a wall between them and God. When something happens or someone hurts them, this person isolates and wants to throw the baby out with the proverbial bathwater. Their heart becomes so hardened and embittered that instead of seeking answers or trying to rebuild, they simply want to light a match to everything they once believed and burn it all down. They're not looking to erase the whiteboard and go back to work; they're just trying to throw it all away.

Perhaps you know someone this has happened to along the way. The Enemy loves it every time this happens and chalks it up as a win. Some within evangelical circles would say the Holy Spirit was never inside the people who denounce their faith. They had never placed their faith in Jesus to begin with, so they are not actually walking away from an authentic faith. Others would disagree with that. Wherever you land, it is no less tragic either way. As people walk away from the faith entirely, the best next step is to consistently share the gospel with them in hopes that they will either genuinely trust in Jesus *or* be reminded of what they once believed in the first place.

Other times people leave the faith because they experience disappointment or grief. Maybe a parent or child dies, they lose a job, they experience a bad breakup, or they get cancer or suffer illness. If this is you, I am so sorry! Every day we come into contact with a world that is fractured and broken, in need of being restored to its original intent. But please don't shake your fist at God as though He inflicted you with loss and disease. God never desired that His children would suffer. We know that because of the fall in Genesis 3 the world is no longer how God intended it to be.

God's first desire is that His children (us!) would dwell with Him in perfect unity and peace. That our hearts would be filled with joy as we're surrounded by perfection. That is what God is moving us toward. But in this middle space of brokenness, the god (little *g*) of this world who tries to steal, kill, and destroy wants to use every bit of suffering to drive a wedge between you and God. He delights when you suffer and delights even more when you blame God for it. This is central to his strategy of keeping you from God.

Another cause of deconstruction the Enemy uses, particularly within my millennial and Gen Z friends, is the perceived hypocrisy they see from Christians. A 2018 Barna research study found that hypocrisy among religious people was the second-leading cause for people in both generations walking away from the faith.[1] As I read that, I can't help but think that behind that are generations of kids who saw their parents play religious games.

They grew up putting on their Sunday best, plastering smiles on their faces, and putting their best foot forward, all while their actual walks with Jesus were merely a facade. So you end up with a whole wave of young adults who think, *I want nothing to do with that.* I frequently try to tell the church I lead that Christianity makes for a terrible hobby. Be all in. Be about the things Jesus was about. But going through the motions year in and year out simply drives out the people who can smell the inauthenticity of your faith from a mile away. And the Enemy loves those kinds of "Christians" because they are the least effective kind. They require little to no effort on his part.

This is also where the idea of "church hurt" comes into play. I hear this phrase so often from people as they disconnect from church. They say that the church hurt them—but, as respectfully as I can say it, I think that is a farce. I understand what people are saying when they say that, but what they mean is, "Someone from a church hurt me." It may have been a fellow member, a small group leader, or a pastor. Or even a group of people. Whoever it was, that person is sinful, not perfect, and is going to let you down in some way. And I'm sorry that it happened to you.

Now, I know grave injustices have been done inside the walls of churches. There has been actual abuse—emotional, physical, spiritual, you name it. I am in no way intending to excuse that! And if that is part of your story, I am so, so sorry. I also know that a lot of people hide behind the phrase "church hurt" when they just don't want to work through conflict with other believers in a biblical way. The best thing to do in that situation is to go to that person, express how they have hurt you, and work through conflict the way Scripture lays out for us.

I have also walked alongside people who stay stuck in an endless loop of questions. Hear me say this: Questions are *not* bad. They are not sinful. They are not wrong. I am not discouraged when people have questions. Questions are great! But I have seen a shift over the last decade where some people only want to live in the questions. Often, these people are not really that interested in finding answers. They don't want you to send them articles to read or podcasts to listen to or scriptures to meditate on, but instead they move on to the next question, then the next, then the next.

Before too long, they have so many different open mental loops that finding the answers is too daunting, so they just open more loops and ask more questions. If you have questions—the age of the earth, what happened to dinosaurs, how the Bible came together—these big-rock questions that you cannot stop thinking about, that's great! But please don't stay in a place where you just have questions and you don't search out the truth. There have never been more resources in the history of history for you to find answers to your questions. Seek out the answers.

Finally, I have witnessed so many people wrestle through these things on their own. They are afraid to ever voice their doubts or questions aloud out of fear of what others might think of them. Please, please, please hear me out on this: Do not go through this process alone. The Enemy loves nothing more than when we isolate and pull back from other believers who can speak truth into our lives. Isolation compounds the problem.

A HEALTHIER WAY TO REBUILD

Kevin is a close friend who walked through his own deconstruction journey over the past few years. Honestly, it felt like it came out of nowhere. It started to mess with his head as he peeled back all the layers of a number of different theological topics that, at one point in his life, he had been certain of. But he didn't try to walk that road alone. He brought his wife in, then he looped in his small group. As days turned into weeks, he had people who loved him and cared for him consistently asking him thoughtful questions and pointing him toward Jesus. And they never gave up on him. They did not excommunicate him or shun him for not just having blind faith.

Over time, Kevin kept coming back to Jesus and the fact that, even if Kevin had questions or doubts, Jesus had changed his life. Finally, he got to the point where, with all integrity, he could say, "People have let me down, but Jesus never let me down." There were times he didn't like what the Bible had to say about a certain topic. He had questions that still felt unanswered at times. But Jesus—the One who died for his sins and made him a new creation—never let him down. With the help of other believers around him, he was able to put his sledgehammer down and start to rebuild. That is a picture of what healthy deconstruction (and reconstruction) looks like.

As I think about what it looks like to follow Jesus for the long haul, I'm reminded of what the author of Hebrews told us toward the end of the book. We don't know who the author of Hebrews was. But what we do know is that the book was written to a church that was growing weary, exhausted, fainthearted. They were beginning to falter in their faith because of the Jewish rules that surrounded them. Here is what they were told:

> Therefore, since we are surrounded by such a great cloud of witnesses, let us throw off everything that hinders and the sin that so easily entangles. And let us run with perseverance the race marked out for us, fixing our eyes on Jesus, the pioneer and perfecter of faith. For the joy set before him he endured

the cross, scorning its shame, and sat down at the right hand of
the throne of God. Consider him who endured such opposition
from sinners, so that you will not grow weary and lose heart.
(Hebrews 12:1–3)

The journey of faith is a long one. It requires perseverance
and other believers alongside us so we don't grow weary and lose
heart along the way. Some of you reading this right now are in a
pit. You feel stuck, like you will be in there forever. You need to
invite people into it with you who will put their arms around you
and help you climb out.

Some of you know someone in that pit, and you need to reach
out to that struggling friend or loved one and let them know they
are not alone. Climb down in with them, put your arm around
them, and say, "Hey, we are going to climb out of here together.
One step at a time. I know you're in a pit. I know you're having a
hard time. I am committed to helping you climb out of here."

This is a picture of what it looks like for the church to be the
church. And there is nothing the Enemy hates more than the
church on the move.

MAKE IT STICK: BUILDING ON JESUS

The best thing you can do if you're in a season of deconstruction and
reconstruction is to keep coming back to Jesus as the foundation of
your faith.

In the space below, reflect on the person of Jesus. Why do you
continue coming back to Jesus? Why do you believe what you believe
about Jesus? What has Jesus done in your life to make you want to
follow Him? Use this space to strengthen your faith.

PART 3

HOW TO FIGHT BACK

GROWING UP, I GOT IN A LOT OF FIGHTS. THIS WAS not ideal for me, because I was not good at fighting. When I say "I got in a lot of fights growing up," that actually means "I got beat up a lot in high school." I was from a small town, but about thirty minutes away was the bigger town of Victoria, where we'd go to the movies, grab some pizza, hang out in the mall, or even go skating (if you're into that). Victoria had it all. In high school, I was kind of a wannabe gangster, which was tough for me to pull off. Turns out that growing up on a farm really hurt my gangster rep (you know, the cows and all).

When my friends and I would go to Victoria, it seemed like I constantly had to look over my shoulder. But somehow, for reasons I still don't understand, I became friends with a guy named Pookie, and whenever he came along to Victoria, I felt safe. He had become a full-grown man when he grew a mustache in the eighth grade, and he could bench-press more than anybody else.

He could beat up anyone, and he proved it a few times, so I always loved when he came to Victoria too.

What does this have to do with spiritual warfare? It's important to remember that you cannot (and will not) defeat the Enemy by yourself. No amount of willpower, no amount of mental toughness, no amount of discipline you can muster completely by yourself can win this battle. In fact, he is bigger than you, smarter than you, and stronger than you. This isn't high school mischief; we are at war with the Prince of Darkness, the one who is responsible for rape, murder, genocide, and every other type of evil out there.

Battling the real Enemy takes the Holy Spirit alive and at work *in* you. By yourself, you are not enough. By yourself, you'd best be scared. Very scared. With the Spirit of God working inside your life, though, the Enemy doesn't stand a chance.

Many of the problems we face today as the global church stem from the fact we have more knowledge at our disposal than any generation before us, but often it ends there. If this book ended after part 2, you would (hopefully) know more information about the Enemy and the war we are in, but it would still leave you right on the sidelines—ineffective. Right where the villain and his forces want you.

To fight back, we need to start by making sure we are doing all the things Christians *should* be doing. We need the armor of God—and this is so much more than the felt-board exercise we learned in Sunday school. It's more than a song, even though we "are in the Lord's army" (*Yes, sir!*). There are real, practical steps that can help us battle back. Additionally, we must pray like crazy, like our lives depend upon it—because our lives do depend on it. We also need to read, learn, and internalize God's Word so we can clash against temptation. And finally, we need to learn how to guard our hearts and keep them away from any and all evil.

My hope is that part 3 of this book is the practical, "aha" section, where everything you have read up to this point starts to come together. Once we understand who our Enemy is and what our Enemy does, the natural progression is to do something about it. But our goal is not just to fight back. Our goal is to fight back and *win*.

CHAPTER 10

THE ARMOR OF GOD

A COUPLE OF YEARS AGO, MY SON, WESTON, HAD a day off school. So I decided to take the day off to hang out with him and do whatever he wanted to do. He wanted to take his scooter up to the skate park and ride around. When he suggested it, it was a proud parent moment. Growing up, I rode my skateboard everywhere I went. We had a little ramp in our backyard and everything. It had been a minute, but I figured it was like riding a bicycle. As soon as we got to the skate park, I would pick up where I left off. Turns out, I was wrong.

We got to the skate park, and I said, "Okay, let's go." But Weston plopped down on the floor. He had to gear up, putting on kneepads, elbow pads, his helmet—you name it, he had protective gear for it. While he methodically (and slowly) put everything on, I went on Instagram and posted about being at the skate park with my boy. Almost immediately people started responding, telling me that I needed a helmet and pads. Did they not know this was my *thing*?

After scrolling through a few replies, I put my phone in my pocket and went for it down a ramp. I kid you not, within about

3.7 seconds of me starting, I fell—hard. I wiped out and was lying there writhing in pain. Weston ran over to check and see if I was okay. Suddenly, I became the spectacle that everyone in the park was watching. *Clearly, they should have a sign posted that this place isn't meant for anyone over the age of forty.*

After my wipeout, I sat down on a bench while Weston continued to ride his scooter. A younger guy, probably in his late twenties, came and sat down next to me. His fingernails were painted black, he was dressed in all black, and he was wearing a crystal around his neck. After a minute or so, I did what I always try to do in those situations. I said, "Hey, do you have a faith?" He then talked for the next thirty minutes, telling me what he believes, which could best be described as a sort of naturalistic mysticism with a dark outer-space twist.

Eventually, once I could get a word in, I asked, "What do you believe about Jesus?" He started talking about his beliefs about Jesus, then he started casually talking about serpents in the wilderness. He was suddenly very coherent, his eyes were clear, and he looked straight at me as he clearly recounted a story from the Bible. He went into detail about the serpents in Numbers 21 when Moses made a bronze snake. He referenced the Rod of Asclepius.

Okay, let me ask you a question, reader. How many times in your life have you had a conversation about the Rod of Asclepius? This is the image often found on the side of an ambulance, with a snake going up a rod. The imagery is based on a pagan retelling of Numbers 21.

Here's why that's crazy. Two weeks earlier, on Easter Sunday, I had preached on Numbers 21 about the fiery serpents, and I mentioned the Rod of Asclepius. Studying for that sermon was the only reason I knew what this guy in the middle of the Waco skate park was talking about. Certainly he had been there, right? No! I was so confused. He moved on and suddenly he was all over the place again. He wouldn't look at me, and I was trying to keep up as he changed directions every few sentences. The conversation turned back to ramblings of mysticism, crystals, galaxies, and starships.

I said, "Wait, go back to Numbers 21. How do you know so much about that chapter?" He looked at me with a blank, ominous stare and slowly said, "What chapter? What is Numbers? Is that in the Bible?" I said, "Wait, what?! Yes! You just told me all about it! The bronze serpent. The Rod of Asclepius?! Remember?! Numbers 21?" He shrugged his shoulders and said, "No, I haven't read far enough in the Bible to get to Numbers yet. I'm not sure what you're talking about." He continued on, rambling for a few more minutes about black magic before hopping back on his board and skating away.

What just happened?!

As I sat there on that stiff wooden bench in the middle of a skate park, I realized that kneepads and elbow pads weren't all I needed that day. I needed the armor of God. You see, what I encountered that day was different.

As you read this, you might be thinking, *Oh, he must have some kind of condition. Maybe schizophrenia or multiple personality disorder.* We love a logical explanation, but trust me: This was different. In that moment as I was about to share the gospel, it was like the Enemy was saying, "I know what you're trying to do here." It was a reminder that this battle is not an earthly one, but a spiritual one. And this stage of the battle was going down in the middle of a skate park.

We shouldn't be surprised. We enter into spiritual warfare the moment we profess faith in Jesus. The moment you say, "Jesus, I trust that You died for my sins and that God raised You from the dead," everything changes. At that moment, you set foot in a battle. You enter into a spiritual conflict that you and I don't think enough about.

The villain is coming after you. He is after your beliefs. He is after your children. He is after your purity. He is after your marriage. He is after your business. Anything he can do to make you unsuccessful, he will do. So you have to be ready. You have to be prepared, because if you aren't prepared, you are going to get hurt.

THE FULL ARMOR OF GOD

If you grew up in church, or even spent much time there as an adult, you have talked about the armor of God. You made the craft in Sunday school. You were in the skit where you put on the oversized helmet. You have heard it. But what does it mean?

The first three chapters in Ephesians are all about who Jesus is and what He's done for us. There are no moral commands in Ephesians 1–3. It is all about Jesus. Then we get to Ephesians 4 and 5, and the word repeated over and over is *walk*. Walk in this way. This is how we walk as followers of Jesus. Finally, when we get to Ephesians 6, the repeated word is *stand*. Whenever we're talking about the spiritual war that we are in, Scripture is constantly commanding, exhorting, and admonishing us to stand firm. To hold our ground and to not be moved.

Ephesians 6:10–12 reads, "Finally, be strong in the Lord and in his mighty power. Put on the full armor of God, so that you can take your stand against the devil's schemes. For our struggle is not against flesh and blood, but against the rulers, against the authorities, against the powers of this dark world and against the spiritual forces of evil in the heavenly realms."

The Holy Spirit, through Paul, was saying to the church in Ephesus, "Nero is not your enemy. The Sanhedrin is not your enemy. The Pharisees are not your enemy. Rome is not your enemy. You have one Enemy, and he is the devil. Satan!" We need to be reminded that our enemy is not the Democrats and it's not the Republicans. The enemy is not your boss, and it is not your angry neighbor. It's not the guy on the road who flipped you off. You only have one Enemy, and he operates through people to discourage you.

If you can just get your head and heart around that idea, you'll fight differently. You'll start to realize, *Oh, this person who just yelled at me and is giving me a piece of their mind with their finger in my chest is not my enemy. There is someone greater than them working through them to discourage me. I have one Enemy, and that is Satan, and the battle is not of flesh and blood.* This is a paradigm-shifting idea for us to understand.

Once Paul told us to put on the "full armor of God," he rattled off a list of what we should do. Reading the list, it can feel abstract. But think about it: Most likely, as he wrote, Paul was chained to some Roman soldier, and he was grappling for an illustration. As he sat imprisoned, he looked at the soldier's armor and started to attach it to ideas to help Christians win the battle. Let's read what he said.

> Stand firm then, with the belt of truth buckled around your waist, with the breastplate of righteousness in place, and with your feet fitted with the readiness that comes from the gospel of peace. In addition to all this, take up the shield of faith, with which you can extinguish all the flaming arrows of the evil one. Take the helmet of salvation and the sword of the Spirit, which is the word of God.
>
> And pray in the Spirit on all occasions with all kinds of prayers and requests. With this in mind, be alert and always keep on praying for all the Lord's people. (Ephesians 6:14–18)

Paul was saying that when the day of evil comes and when the

Enemy attacks you, you can do these things to defeat the Enemy. When he comes after you, you will be able to stand your ground. If you want to win against the Enemy, do these things.

Friends, this is the classic spiritual warfare chapter. It is a helpful framework and checklist for you to think through as you fight the Enemy. If you ask any mature Christian familiar with the Bible where it talks about spiritual warfare, they will typically take you to Ephesians 6. This biblical chapter is intense. It is important. And it all begins with knowing the truth.

THE BELT OF TRUTH

The first instruction is to stand firm with the belt of truth buckled around your waist. This is Paul saying, "You need to know what is true and what is not." Many battles have been fought over real estate—an effort to control a territory. The spiritual war is fought over the real estate of your mind. The Enemy is after your *thinking.* He wants to bend the truth and distort the facts. The Enemy's MO is to discourage you—to remove courage from you.

If the villain and his forces can discourage you, you are weak and unable to fight back. You are impotent and not a threat to him any longer. You will be on the sidelines. A weapon he uses here is the weapon of guilt and shame. He comes behind you and says, "You don't belong in a church. You can't sing that song. You can't pray that prayer. You can't read your Bible, you hypocrite. Don't you remember what you did last night (or last week, or last year)?" At our worst, we believe it. And it is *not* the truth.

This is something I am so passionate about: Your Sunday morning worship service is not enough. Your quiet time is not a passive thirty-minute Bible study as you sip your coffee. Reorienting your mind around what is true cannot be contained to small chunks of time; it has to be a constant, daily process where you are filling your mind with truth. The scriptures you read, the podcasts you listen to, and the worship songs you sing as you go about your day are all helpful tools as you focus your mind on the things of God.

This is what it means to wear the belt of truth.

GAIN A HEART OF RIGHTEOUSNESS

The breastplate protects the vital organ of the heart. Paul was telling us here what we need in order to gain a heart of righteousness. We, as Christians, believe that Christ's righteousness is *imputed* upon us. *Imputed* is a churchy word that just means "attributed." Think about it in school terms: If we are turning in a term paper, we are turning in Jesus' grade. We get to point to His report card. We believe that we are going to be measured by Jesus' work, right? And so we have His righteousness. It is mind-blowing!

This begs the question, How should we live? Well, we follow the ways of Jesus. We do what Jesus would have us do. This is so important in every situation for the rest of our lives. For as long as we live, no matter how hard it is, no matter what it costs us or how difficult, we just do what Jesus would have us do. Simple concept. There is a reason those WWJD bracelets exploded in popularity back in the day like they did. We need reminders of what righteousness looks like: Jesus. To be righteous is to conduct ourselves in the same way that Jesus would. Oftentimes in Scripture, righteousness and wickedness are used as contrasting ideas.

Some people on earth are committed to doing wrong. They see the world as their playground. These people have no regard for others. They use others for their own advantage. They will exploit people and situations to get a leg up on the competition. They just want to be happy and experience their own pleasure. And you are just a pawn on their chessboard, right? Not so with followers of Jesus.

We serve people. We love people. We use everything that has been entrusted to us to care for people. We open our homes and show hospitality to everyone. We care for widows and orphans. We don't view relationships as transactional, but as opportunities to see life transformation happen. Some of you may be thinking, *I have never met someone like that.* Then maybe you have never met a Christian. I don't know what else to tell you. That is simply how followers of Jesus lived back then, and it is how we are to live today.

When you gain a heart of righteousness, it changes your life.

STAND ON THE GOSPEL

Next, Paul instructed the Ephesians to have their feet vigilantly planted on the foundation of the gospel. In the Greek, the word for *readiness* is a "prepared foundation." It's what you stand on. The gospel is your foundation—in everything you do. The way that you get from death to life is Jesus.

Here is the thing with the Christian faith: The second you trust in Christ, you step into a fight, a battle, a war. The paradox is that we are at war *and* we have peace. On the surface, that doesn't make sense. It transcends all understanding that we can have peace and be at war.

Why? Most soldiers will tell you their greatest fear is a lethal blow. Every day they're deployed, they're reminded of the stakes everywhere they look. The threat of death looms and hovers around them. But as Christians fighting this spiritual war, we are immortal. Let me tell you two realities. First, if you are a follower of Jesus, you will not die one second before the Lord has ordained. Not one moment.

Second, death is the beginning of the beginning for you. It is a new beginning, where you wake up in paradise with God. That is the hope and reality that we exist in. If that is what we know, then truly, what can the Enemy do to us? That is what it means to have our feet fitted with readiness.

In 1 Peter 3:15, Peter exhorted, "Always be prepared to give an answer to everyone who asks you to give the reason for the hope that you have. But do this with gentleness and respect." Having the peace that comes from the gospel in an anxious world is going to confuse the people who have not trusted in Jesus yet. Peter told us to always be ready to explain why we can be so hopeful. This is what it looks like to be ready.

HOLD ON TO FAITH

A shield for a Roman soldier was a big wooden thing that covered about two-thirds of his body. The way you would defeat a soldier with a wooden shield was with a flaming arrow. If you hit the shield with a flaming arrow, it became kindling. So, Romans would cover the shield with a piece of leather. They would soak the leather in water to make it deflect and extinguish the flaming arrows.[1]

Paul used the Roman shield as a metaphor of how to protect ourselves from the fiery arrows flying our direction. Faith can be difficult at times. The Enemy wants us to doubt and despair. Sometimes it's easy to hold up our shields, but other times it's not. A long line of heroes of the faith have suffered from deep, dark depression and "dark nights of the soul." C. S. Lewis, Charles Spurgeon, Mother Teresa—all experienced a dark time to some degree.[2] Lewis wrote *A Grief Observed* in the aftermath of his wife's death as he grieved. Martin Luther's dark time was well documented. There were times he felt like he couldn't even get out of bed.

Luther said everything turned around for him when he began to see the burden of suffering as a blessing.[3] That was when he began to see the light at the end of the tunnel. He had the realization that, "Oh, the Enemy's after me because God wants to use me." Then he began to reflect on, meditate on, and contemplate the truth. He would put Bible verses to tunes of songs and would sing the truth as a way to hold on to his faith. He turned his suffering into motivation to do something, and we are still talking about it centuries later.

I don't know what is going to help you hold on to faith if and when you experience a dark time, but *you* need to figure out what will help you. Maybe it's journaling or listing out your prayers to see the ones God has answered over the years. Perhaps you need to write your own songs based on Scripture. Learn to do whatever you can to hold on to the shield of faith so the Enemy's arrows are extinguished as they come toward you.

BE MINDFUL OF SALVATION

Paul said in Ephesians 6:17 to "take the helmet of salvation." I believe he was instructing us to be mindful of salvation.

What's the most important piece of protective equipment? The helmet. This is true in the skate park, on a bicycle, in a football game, and in a spiritual battle. The brain is the command center for everything in your body; everything you say and do happens as a result of your brain. If you are in battle and your brain goes down, it is game over. If we are mindful of our salvation, that means we are confident in our salvation. Then all the other actions of a disciple flow out of that.

As a pastor, I have a lot of conversations with people wavering in their faith and questioning their salvation. This is a brilliant trick from the Enemy, because it keeps us from going all in and living fully devoted lives. When we have confidence and assurance, we live confidently as Christ followers.

What's it like when we waver on our salvation? We say things like, "Well, I'm just not sure. I'm just not sure if I am saved." Friends, if you have trusted in Jesus Christ, His death, and His resurrection for the forgiveness of your sins, you are secure; you are saved. Salvation means you are going to be with God forever. And that means you live, move, and speak in this world through Jesus. You see everything through the lens of going to be with God forever.

This gives you what I call the vacation mentality. We are different when we are going on vacation the next day, right? It doesn't matter if the copy machine is on fire or the stock is plummeting, if we are going on vacation the next day, bad news just hits differently. When I'm about to go on vacation, my mind is on vacation. I'm not going to get sucked into the worries of that week. Salvation means that we are about to go on an eternal vacation. We're going to be with God forever and ever and ever in paradise. We have to stay mindful of what salvation is and the implications for us.

HAVE THE WORD READY

When Paul talked about the sword of the Spirit, he was telling us to have the Word of God ready. Now, if you have studied this text or heard it taught on a Sunday morning, you know I am supposed to say it's the only offensive weapon—and that is true. All other pieces of armor are protective gear. The sword of the Spirit is how you attack the Enemy.

What did Paul mean by the sword of the Spirit? It is sixty-six books that were written over fifteen hundred years by forty different authors on multiple continents in three languages with one central truth: God wins. He gets His children back, He defeats the Enemy, and He tells us how to be victorious in our lives. We need to know the Bible and be equipped with it. We are operating in a battle. Make sure you have your sword.

Have you ever had that dream where you show up to school naked? There you are. Suddenly, it hits you: *I forgot to put on clothes.* Some of you are leaving the house with just your helmet of salvation on, but no other clothes. Now, don't get hung up on the metaphor here. But that is your spiritual reality.

It always baffles me how people can be in church for decades and not know anything of substance about the Bible. They view the Old Testament as an outdated history and rulebook, not realizing that it sets up the need for Jesus to come in the first place. We don't know how to navigate it, how to get around it, what it says, what it teaches, or what we should do with it.

You might say, "I've been a Christian for a long time, but I've never learned my Bible." Well, you are not a very effective Christian. You are no threat to the devil. You're unarmed. I'm not saying that to shame you or bring about condemnation; it's a statement of fact. Without an understanding of God's Word, you're going to be ineffective in fighting a spiritual battle of this significance.

In Matthew 4, Jesus came face-to-face with Satan—not just some demon—and was tempted after forty days of fasting. Satan tempted Jesus with His greatest earthly natural desires. Jesus was hungry. He had not eaten for forty days. And Satan said, "Here's some food." Jesus responded with scriptures that He had memorized. In short, Jesus was modeling for us what it looks like to use the sword of the Spirit. This is how we win against the Enemy. We pull Scripture and use it as a way to proactively fight against sin and temptation presented to us by the Enemy. We do this, and we will win.

I'm going to be even more precise with you: Without your sword, you will either lose or you will never get in the game. The Enemy will destroy you or leave you completely alone because you are zero threat to evil. If you are stuck in a life of comfort, the villain and his forces will huddle up. "That one? We don't need to mess with that one. He's not even a threat to what we are doing here. Let's not waste our time." The better option is getting in the battle and winning because you are equipped to do so. You know the Word. You need to have a death grip on the truth and respond with what is true.

After all the equipping with the "full armor of God," the last thing Paul said was, "pray . . . on all occasions" (Ephesians 6:18). Prayer is such an important yet often overlooked facet of our spiritual battle. It is available to all of us, yet so often we fail to wrap our hearts around the importance of it. In the next chapter, we're going to dive deep into the topic of prayer. I'm convinced: If we will commit to prayer, we will loosen the Enemy's grip in a whole new way.

MAKE IT STICK: WEAPON INVENTORY

What element of armor do you feel you are missing in this season?

Which one seems most important to you?

The passage calls us to pray, so let's do that together:

Father, please protect me from the devil and the demons that seek to come after me.

Please cancel any satanic assignment against me, in Jesus' name.

Amen 2/6/25

—my family
—friends
—church
— community & country

    Please bind any demonic works against me, in Jesus' name.

    Please help me to operate in faith and give thanks for my salvation, which is a gift from You.

    Please help me to walk in righteousness.

    Please help me to know the truth at all times, to be ready to share the gospel with anyone who hasn't heard it, and to strengthen the faith of those who have.

    Help me to know Your Word and live in Your peace.

    Thank You for Your protection, Lord. In Jesus' name, amen.

CHAPTER 11

WALKIE-TALKIE PRAYERS

SINCE I ENTERED THE PROFESSIONAL WORKFORCE a couple of decades ago, the way we all communicate with each other has drastically changed. When I first started working, if you wanted to get ahold of someone you simply called their office number. Maybe you would get the assistant and they would write a message on a Post-it Note and walk it back to their boss's office. I worked in sales, so my day was filled with hundreds of cold calls. I was the guy interrupting your family's dinner to try and pitch you a new internet provider. (Sorry about that, by the way.)

As time went on, the game changed. We became an email culture. Everything was done via email. I was good at staying on top of my inbox, and I learned the art of the quick reply. Our whole staff was really efficient at the use of email. Now, if you really needed something done, you always had the option of the phone call. Or, if it was a sensitive discussion, a face-to-face conversation was in order. But often an email would get the job done.

When I moved to Waco, one of my first observations with

the church staff was that I had just entered into a texting culture. Email was secondary. I quickly found myself as a member of a couple dozen group chats—clever names, funny group photos, and all. The staff was a size where everybody could fit into a group text, but it was easy to fall behind really quickly. Then there were other group texts with smaller teams. Then the elders. Then my small group. Then miscellaneous coworkers, church members, friends—you name it. I was in a group text with all of them.

With all these different ways to communicate, constant communication has become normalized. We have social media, we have phones we are glued to, we have email accounts, plus actual face-to-face conversations that happen with people all the time. We have normalized constant interaction, which is not necessarily a bad thing. But here's the thing: We are quick to stay in a never-ending group text with our friends and pass memes back and forth, but slow to spend any significant amount of time in prayer—communing with the God who holds the world in His hand. That's not just some kind of pastoral Jesus-juke; it's just true.

We've talked about this already: The villain loves for us to live hurried, distracted lives. He wants nothing more than for our minds to wander to our to-do list every time we sit down to pray. He wants us to wear the anxiety and cares of the world instead of taking those before the Father. He wants prayer to be an afterthought or a last-ditch effort—like a Hail Mary at the end of a football game.

When I read the Scriptures, I see how they highlight just how much we have missed the mark on prayer. For so many of us, prayer has become confined to a short exercise of discipline that we do in the mornings or before bed, or maybe before a meal. Hear me say this: None of these things are bad. Discipline is required of the Christian. We need regular rhythms when it comes to living out the Scriptures. I am *not* telling you to stop setting aside time to pray. I *am* going to encourage you to make it so much more than that, because that is what I read in the Scriptures.

We find more than 650 different recorded prayers in the Scriptures, including twenty-five different instances of Jesus praying.[1] Sometimes we see prayers of thanksgiving, thanking God for all He has done. Other times we see prayers of lament, mourning, and grieving over the state of the world or a situation. Other times we see prayers of confession and repentance. In some cases, we even see Jesus teaching His followers *how* to pray. Any way you look at it, the often-praying Christian is not meant to be the exception, but the norm.

If you're going to fight a villain stronger than you, you must find someone stronger than him. It's the only way you will ever win. The way you defeat an Enemy stronger than you is finding someone stronger than the Enemy. Because of the crucifixion and resurrection of Jesus, we have access to God. In the Old Testament temple, a curtain, or veil, served as a barrier between God and His people, but that is gone now (it tore at the crucifixion, according to Matthew 27:51). I want us to examine how many of us are praying today and see how we can shift our perspective to a more biblical way of praying. If you ask God, "Why did you let Satan attack me?" could He respond, "You didn't ask Me to protect you"?

WARTIME PRAYERS VERSUS ROOM-SERVICE PRAYERS

A vision that I cast for our staff at the church is walkie-talkie communication, a term I learned somewhere along the way that speaks to me. Since we are all locking arms and trying to push back against the spiritual darkness in our city and world, it is important that we master the art of communication with one another as we shepherd people together. Now, how we communicate matters less than the frequency of our communication. The principle is clear: When fighting a battle, walkie-talkie communication matters.

On the battlefield, you don't always have time for a strategic communication plan. As bullets are whizzing by, things may not go exactly as you planned. There's no time to huddle up and strategize. You are grabbing your walkie-talkie and giving instructions. You're asking where to go, or telling someone else where you're going, so they know. It's constant and it's practiced often so, in the heat of battle and the fog of war, you are not caught vulnerable and flat-footed by your enemy. Communication on the walkie-talkies is literally a matter of life and death.

As the Enemy comes at you with destruction, distraction, deception, disunity, desensitization, and deconstruction to rob you of a life following Jesus, what does your prayer life look like? When one of those six things hits you, how do you respond? Is your gut instinct to start begging the very God who has all the authority in the world to step in on your behalf, or do you try to pull yourself up and hope you can handle it all on your own? The answer to those questions teaches us a lot about our theology, whether we realize it or not.

When Monica and I got married, we went on our honeymoon to an all-inclusive resort in Mexico. This kind of vacation was a first for me. I couldn't believe it! Not only could we order whatever we wanted at one of the seven restaurants, we could order room service at any time. I could pick up the phone, push a button, and on the other end of the line I would hear, "Good day, Mr. Pokluda! This is room service. How may I help you?" What?! I could get used to this! I could ask them for whatever I wanted, whenever I wanted! Here's what was true: When I wanted something, I called. I didn't, however, talk to them nonstop. There was no reason to. I didn't always want or need something.

I have heard pastor John Piper explain this by saying that far too often we fall into the trap of limiting our prayers, as if God is like a heavenly room-service attendant and we're calling to see if we can get some chocolate cake at 11:00 p.m.[2] We think, *Look at this menu of things we want here on this earth. He can bring this to me.* We pray for spouses, new jobs, children, new houses, new friends, and hope that the message of what we want makes it to God.

Should we pray for the desires of our hearts? Absolutely we should. I'm not telling you we should not ask in full faith and confidence for those things (the Scriptures say we should in texts like Matthew 7:7 and Mark 11:24). But we don't need to put an artificial ceiling on those prayers, where all we're doing is going to God with our selections from a menu.

My uncle refers to these as "We Just" prayers, where we say things like, "God, we just want Your presence" or "Father, we just would love it if You would do just this one thing." I think it is a fair criticism of how we pray. Nowhere does Scripture tell us to hedge our prayers or that God has a limited capacity for what He may or may not want to do as a result of our petitions. Do you want people to come to know Jesus? Who? Everyone? Why not ask God, "Please save every human being on earth" every day? Our "big asks" of God are still far too small.

We can get a mental block somewhere in our subconscious that we are bothering God if we pray for too many things at once. I don't know who needs to read this, but don't believe that God is sitting in conference room meetings in heaven and stepping out to see that He is a few million messages behind, and He is going to never get around to reading all but the few most recent arrivals. He is more omnipotent and omnipresent than our minds can fathom. He hears our prayers. Every single one of them. If He is bothered by them at all, I'm convinced it would only be because our requests are too few and too small.

Wartime prayers are different. They happen by necessity. They must be impromptu, efficient, constant—like your life depends upon them. What does a walkie-talkie prayer look like? That's when you pull into the Starbucks parking lot and say, "God, who in there do you want me to share the gospel with?" As you see your lost neighbor in their front yard and say, "Hey, I'm going over there, Lord. How do You want to bring Your kingdom into this situation?" As you go to pick up your kids from school and say, "I'm sitting in the carpool line. Who's in front of me? Who's behind me, God? What do You want me to do?" If you are a student you say, "I'm in second period, God. The wildest kid in the whole school is in here. What do You want me to do, God? How can I partner with You?" You pray things like, "Father, I know I have an Enemy; please protect me from him. Please make my ears deaf to his lies. Please make my thoughts fixed on what brings glory to You."

Perhaps this is a completely different mindset than what you are used to. There's a reason the apostle Paul instructed the Thessalonians to "pray continually" (1 Thessalonians 5:17). If the villain had it his way, he would love for you to do everything by your own strength with no reliance on the Holy Spirit whatsoever. Since I've become more intentional about praying walkie-talkie prayers, I've seen a noticeable shift in my own heart posture.

On a day when I am fully surrendered to the Spirit, I am communicating with God all throughout the day. I'm asking for wisdom as I walk into a conversation with a member of the church. I'm asking for humility as I look for ways to sacrificially serve my wife. I'm praying for patience on the drive home, so I can be the fully present and attentive father my kids need. In a moment of temptation, when I feel the urge to buy that thing or click on that hashtag, I default to a conversation with God.

Prayer can be the first and last thing we do in every and any situation. I have found myself asking people to pray *for me* before I even pray about it myself. How confusing is that? Prayer is just as accessible to me as it is to the people I just asked for prayer. This is a battle, and we are all on the front lines. We must communicate like it.

LISTENING FOR GOD

We established that it is imperative for us to be talking to God constantly, but what about listening? If you were to assess your own prayer life, how skilled are you at hearing from God?

Here's what I have seen over time, through thousands and thousands of case studies right in front of me: The closer someone is walking with Jesus, the more in tune with the voice of God they are going to be. Hundreds of times, I have had the same conversation with people at the front of the stage after a message. They say something like, "I'm just not hearing from God right now." I always ask a follow-up: "Are you listening for Him?"

This is where the tactic of distraction is most at war with our prayer life. Our society has trained us to find it next to impossible to be still and silent. Try setting aside one whole minute of silence next time you are in a room of people. It will feel like thirty, because we are so used to noise. And the Enemy loves the chaos— the mental checklists and to-do lists that take up so much of our minds. The simple act of sitting in silence to listen for the voice of God runs directly in contrast to every time waster the Enemy would love to put in front of us.

A couple of years ago, our church needed to make some decisions regarding land expansion and future direction. We had a lot of options, and the list of things we *could* do felt endless, so we were on a mission to find out what we *should* do. In that process, our elders read a book called *Chair Time* by Dan Southerland.[3] It is a short read, and the premise is simple: The best way to hear from God is to eliminate all distractions and simply sit and listen. We started an experiment and invited others in the church to join us. For thirty days, we set aside fifteen minutes a day to simply sit and listen to God.

Now, on the surface, fifteen minutes doesn't sound like a terribly long time. That's about as much as a rerun episode of *Friends* without commercials. But when the assignment is fifteen minutes with no Bible, no journal, no music, no memory verses, and no talking, fifteen minutes can feel like an eternity. In the beginning, I was discouraged at how quickly my mind could wander all over the map. But over time, as I grew in the discipline of sitting, I became more skilled at a quick prayer to refocus my mind on the exercise: listening.

Going into the thirty-day experiment, my hope was that all of us (or at the very least, one of us) would have a grand revelation where we heard the audible voice of God tell us exactly what we should do. I don't believe that happened to anyone. But the unintended reward (at least for me) was that I became more in tune with the voice of God throughout the day. I could feel the Spirit telling me what to do, what to say and not say, and how to react in ways I had not before, all because I had grown in the discipline of listening.

The better we are at listening to the Spirit, the more easily we can discern what is of God and what is of the Enemy. Richard Foster, in his book *Celebration of Discipline*, makes this observation about Jesus and His followers:

Perhaps the most astonishing characteristic of Jesus' praying is that when he prayed for others he *never* concluded by saying, "If it be thy will." Nor did the apostles or prophets when they were praying for others. They obviously believed that they knew what the will of God was before they prayed the prayer of faith. They were so immersed in the milieu of the Holy Spirit that when they encountered a specific situation, they knew what should be done. Their praying was so positive that it often took the form of a direct, authoritative command: "Walk," "Be well," "Stand up." I saw that when praying for others there was evidently no room for indecisive, tentative, half-hoping, "If it be thy will" prayers.[4]

So much of our prayer life is consumed by trying to discern God's will, but that is next to impossible to do when we have fragmented minds and hearts. Fighting back against the Enemy becomes a whole lot easier when we eliminate the guesswork of "What should I do in this situation?" The closer we are walking alongside Jesus, the more clearly we will know the right next step in each situation we find ourselves in.

PSYCHOLOGY AND PRAYER

We have touched sporadically throughout this book on the link between the Enemy and his desire to attack our thoughts. I would be remiss to not discuss the importance of prayer when it comes to those of you who are in a dark place mentally. Since 2017 and 2018 when I faced my own battle with a serious case of anxiety, I have been fascinated with psychology. I have always been interested in how the mind works, but during that season, I started deep-diving into what was going on in modern psychology and studying the effects of cognitive behavioral therapy (CBT). I wanted to better understand how the mind works and how it ultimately drives our behavior.

Do you know what I have found? In many ways, there's nothing new under the sun (as Solomon would say). As it turns out, the Bible is a fantastic book on psychology, the human psyche, and how to rightly understand our outlook and perspective. Every couple of years, it seems like there is a new breakthrough in modern psychology that Scripture has been speaking to for a few thousand years.

Ten to twenty years ago, you would go to see a therapist or counselor and say, "Hey, I'm struggling with depression or anxiety." They could recommend a psychiatrist or your doctor who would give you what is known as an SSRI (a selective serotonin reuptake inhibitor). Now, this is not a statement about medication. I have no issue with following a trusted doctor's instructions, and medication has been very helpful to some people. But an interesting shift has taken place in the world of mental health today: If you walk into a therapist's office and say, "I am struggling with anxiety or depression," their first action step will likely be to prescribe you something that looks a whole lot like prayer. Not you asking God to remove your anxiety, but deep reflection and holding thoughts in your mind. They might call it "mindfulness" or meditation.

A secular professional may say, "Here's what I want you to do. I want you to start every day by sitting still and thinking about all the blessings or good things in your life. Fixate on each one of them. Learn to really meditate on those thoughts. When an unhelpful thought enters your mind, take it captive by observing it, rejecting it, and moving back to the positive thoughts, and hold on to them throughout the day. Remember: Give careful consideration to what you allow into your brain." I have practiced CBT myself and found it to be useful. And even while doing it, I realized it felt a whole lot like prayer. It feels like someone went back in time and cracked open the book of Psalms, where David spoke on the importance of meditating on God's Word both day and night (Psalm 1:2).

Recently I was talking to a friend who, over time, had lost his way. He left Jesus' path for a little while. The Enemy had robbed him of his joy and purpose. He was overtaken by insecurity, depression, and harmful thoughts. His life spiraled, and if you knew him, you could see it in his eyes. One day we were talking about the journey he had been on and he said, "You know, prayer healed me."

Honestly, I was taken aback because I did not expect to hear that from him. Then he said, "But not that the prayer was answered. The activity of sitting alone with God every morning and just fixating on the things above, reflecting on what He has done, thinking about the cross, the empty tomb, heaven forever and ever and ever, and filling my heart with hope moved me to a better place."

If you are in a similar place, I am so sorry. I know that's so difficult. I also want to beg you to return to prayer. I've seen it repeatedly: Your heart might be reluctant to do it, but it can heal you.

WHAT IF?

Let me present you with a hypothetical situation. Can you imagine if God showed up and answered all your prayers today? If God showed up today and said, "Hi, I'm God. All your prayers are answered." What would change? For some of us, the only thing that would change would be that we would simply be a better us. You might have more money, a nicer house, and better-behaved children.

For some of you, He would show up and say, "Hey, I just

answered all your prayers." You would say, "Really? What did you do?" He would say, "I'm here! That's what you asked for. That I would be here. Here I am! Every day all you asked for was that I would be with you, so here I am!" Some of us devote our entire prayer lives to asking for God's presence, but if we have the Holy Spirit, He has already done that.

So that's the question I want to leave you with. What would change if all your prayers were answered? I am convinced, the longer I follow Jesus and pastor others who do the same, that prayer is one of the greatest indicators of faith we have. I'm talking about prayers of solitude when you are all by yourself. I am talking about the walkie-talkie prayers as you fight the Enemy on the battlefield every day. I am talking about when you stop in the middle of the grocery store to pray for a stranger because you felt the Spirit's prompting.

Here's my hunch: If we really want to push back against all the most common tactics of the Enemy, we must start and end with prayer. We need to boldly pray every day, in the name of Jesus, by His authority, that the Enemy would be defeated. We need to pray with the belief that God can and wants to answer every prayer we pray. If we want the full and abundant life that comes with following Jesus, prayer must be our starting point.

MAKE IT STICK: RUNNING PRAYER LIST

Try living a full day, from the time you wake up to the time you go to bed, keeping track of all your walkie-talkie prayers. At the end of the day, count up your prayers. How many people and situations were you able to pray about or pray for today?

Pro-tip: Start by looking at your calendar or planner to see what you have on your schedule for the day. Begin by praying for each appointment on your calendar to prepare your heart for what God has in store for you.

CHAPTER 12

RESISTING TEMPTATION

EVERY YEAR, I GIVE SOMETHING UP ON JANUARY 1 for the duration of the year. In an effort to not be mastered by anything, I have found it is a helpful practice to go a year without something. Over the years, I have given up sodas, buying things for myself, coffee, and dessert. Now, it's important for you to know that I love desserts. I always have since I was little, and I don't discriminate. I know some of you are thinking, *Oh yeah, I love sweets. I can't turn down cookies. That's kind of my thing.* But we are not the same.

Cookies are my thing, cake is my thing, pie is my thing, doughnuts are my thing, and candy is my thing. If it has sugar, I'm way into it. I love all kinds of candy: hard candy, soft candy, and candy that has stuff inside of it. Any kind of candy, unless it has coconut (because then it is basically a chocolate-covered salad).

Here's a public service announcement: As I have gotten older, my metabolism has slowed down. That happens. Some of you know what I am talking about. The part of your body that burns fat starts pumping the brakes. I started to wear the candy, if you will. So the decision to give up sweets for a year was both an act of discipline *and* an opportunity to be healthier all at the same time.

My friend Scott and I agreed on a challenge. We said, "We're going to do one year with no desserts." For added accountability, we added in a financial component. The bet was if I ate a dessert, I had to give him one hundred dollars, and the same went for Scott. We had to have some skin in the game. We shook on it like men and began our quest.

As soon as I shook his hand on this deal and said, "Okay, I'm in, no desserts for one year," desserts started showing up out of nowhere. I mean, sweets just magically appeared. People were dropping off brownies, bringing by bowls of candy, like "Hey, my wife just made these cookies. You're going to hurt her feelings if you don't eat one." Everywhere I turned, somebody was offering me some kind of free dessert. Everybody was in on this temptation game.

One night sticks out. Sometimes when I speak somewhere, the organizers might give me a gift card as a thank-you once it's over. With one speaking engagement, I got a gift card to a really nice restaurant, and Monica and I saved it to celebrate our anniversary. We went and had an amazing meal. Great conversation, great food, great time together. The perfect night.

After we finished eating and were ready for the bill, I got my gift card out. The server came by and said some kind things. He said, "Hey, we have never met, but I have been impacted by your ministry. God has done a work in my life. I would love to do something special for you as a small way to thank you." He then set in front of me a giant piece of chocolate cake. Not a small slice. This cake had many, many layers. There I was just staring at it, conflicted about what I should do. In hindsight, I probably responded weirdly because my eyes got big and I said, "Oh no." Then I regained my composure and said, "That's so kind; thank you so much. Did Scott put you up to this?"

As he walked away and I just sat there staring at the cake, Monica said, "What are you going to do?" I said, "Well I guess I am going to pay Scott a hundred dollars." And let me tell you, it was worth every dollar.

This is a picture of how temptation works. We resolve to abstain from something—to say "no more!"—and try and move in a different direction. As soon as we make that decision, whatever we just gave up starts to present itself out of nowhere. The villain loves to tempt us.

Here's a helpful, simple working definition of *temptation*: a proposition to not trust God. Anytime you're given choices and one of those choices is to *not* trust God—that is temptation. Whenever you can choose between a set of options and one of those options is to trust your feelings, your thoughts, your desires, your logic, or whatever else the Enemy wants to use to tempt you— that is temptation.

People fall all across the spectrum when it comes to fighting the temptations of the villain. Some of you are walking by the Holy Spirit, resisting temptation, and you are finding victory. Praise God for that! In James 4:7, the Bible says that if we stand firm and resist the Enemy, the Enemy will flee from us. Some of you are actively resisting temptation, even when it appears on a (metaphorical) plate right in front of you. A villain is actively trying to get you to sin. He's serving up cake when you're trying to go without. Some of you are in the fight. You are aware of the temptations in front of you and sometimes you resist them, but other times you give yourself over to them. You have periods of resistance and victory, followed by seasons of succumbing to the Enemy's wishes. How do I know this? Because this is me.

Some of you may even be starting to feel like victory is impossible and you are wearing your sin as if it is some kind of modern-day scarlet letter. You think, *I guess I'll just always struggle with porn*, or *Alcohol will just always be my ditch*, and you have accepted defeat. But I am here to tell you that it doesn't have to be that way.

It's important to remember that temptation itself is not sinful. The temptation is not what drives a wedge between you and God—sin is. Too often we find ourselves tempted in a situation and we go down a mental rabbit hole where we beat ourselves up for being tempted, when it is completely normal and a tactic the Enemy uses to pull us toward sin. The skill we need to develop as we grow in maturity in our relationship with Jesus is the ability to *resist* temptation. There is no better playbook for us to follow when fighting temptation than the one given to us by Jesus Himself.

HOW JESUS FOUGHT BACK

At the end of Matthew 3, Jesus was baptized. This was the beginning of his public ministry. We don't have a ton of information about the life of Jesus prior to this moment. He was baptized, the Holy Spirit descended on Him like a dove, and the voice of God said, "This is my Son . . . with him I am well pleased" (v. 17). God told those present that this was His Son, and now the earthly ministry of Jesus was about to take off. Then something strange happened at the beginning of Matthew 4. It reads, "Then Jesus was led by the Spirit into the wilderness to be tempted by the devil" (v. 1).

Wait, what? Why would God do that? Why would God even allow Satan to tempt Jesus? There are a couple of reasons. One is so we can see He was tempted in every way but did not sin (Hebrews 4:15–16). God was giving us an example and giving us hope that we can follow in Jesus' footsteps. The second reason is to display to us *how* to resist temptation. Jesus gave us the secret so that for the rest of our lives, we will know how to fight back against the Enemy's temptations. Jesus showed us how we can resist the devil.

As we briefly touched on in chapter 10, the Scriptures tell us that after forty days and forty nights Jesus was hungry, which makes perfect sense. Anytime you fast for more than a handful of hours, you end up hungry. It checks out that after forty days, Jesus was really hungry. He was vulnerable, so it was a logical time for the villain to swoop in, which is exactly what happened. "The tempter came to him and said, 'If you are the Son of God, tell the stones to become bread.' Jesus answered, 'It is written: "Man shall not live on bread alone, but on every word that comes from the mouth of God"'" (Matthew 4:3–4).

Satan is the tempter. He showed up and appealed to Jesus' wants and desires. He said, "I know you are hungry." The villain tried to get Jesus to doubt God. He enticed Him with the very thing he knew Jesus wanted. We have already established that if we crack open that door, we give the Enemy a foothold. He sticks his foot in and says, "Can I come in?" But you can say, "I'm not going to do that," as Jesus modeled for us here.

Notice what Jesus did. He responded to Satan's efforts with Scripture. And not just any scripture. He responded by quoting Deuteronomy 8:3. In fact, all three times Jesus was tempted in this passage, He responded to the Enemy by quoting from Deuteronomy—specifically a passage about the importance of following God's instructions.

Remember: Jesus had not eaten in forty days. The desire of His flesh, in that moment, would be to eat anything and everything put in front of Him. It is at that point that the Enemy came and said, "Why don't you eat that?" He didn't come on day eight. He didn't come in the middle of His fasting. He came at the lowest moment, the most difficult time when Jesus was at His weakest. But at the same time, we need to keep this in mind: Jesus had just gotten baptized.

This story gives us a picture of how the Enemy comes for us at our highest and lowest points. Jesus was coming off this spiritual mountaintop moment where He was baptized and was preparing for ministry, but then He was hungry in the desert. The Enemy doesn't care; he will come at you in the high and lows.

Everything in the humanity of Jesus would have agreed with Satan: "I'm hungry and I want food." But it was not the will of His Father, so He didn't do it. What was the will of His Father? That He would be hungry and without food during this preparatory fast. Why? So those desires and urges would be turned into a dependence on His Father.

Countless times in ministry I've talked with people struggling with some particular sin or desire or coping mechanism. They will tell me, "Well, JP, if God didn't want me to do this, He wouldn't have given me these desires. If He didn't want me to do that, I wouldn't feel this way."

Let me be abundantly clear with you: You 100 percent, without a doubt, unequivocally have desires that God does not want you to act on. I have desires to do and say all kinds of things that are inconsistent with God's Word. For some things you want, you should put those desires to death and not follow them. You should resist. You should stand strong. You should be disciplined and say, "I am not going to just follow every inkling of a desire within my body. I need to fast and trust His Word rather than follow my wants." It's difficult, but it's exactly what God wants from us in that moment.

THE ALLURE OF POWER

As the story continues, Satan kept putting opportunities in front of Jesus for Him to model what it looks like to fight the temptations of the Enemy. Here's what happens next in this story:

> Then the devil took him to the holy city and had him stand on the highest point of the temple. "If you are the Son of God," he said, "throw yourself down. For it is written:
>
> "'He will command his angels concerning you, and they will lift you up in their hands, so that you will not strike your foot against a stone.'"
>
> Jesus answered him, "It is also written: 'Do not put the Lord your God to the test.'" (Matthew 4:5–7)

Here the Enemy was trying to tempt Jesus again. He was saying, "Prove you are the Son of God. Prove it to me, and prove it to them." You see, in Malachi 3, the prophet said that the Messiah (Jesus) would descend upon the temple. So the Jews of this day had been watching the temple. They were watching the sky around the temple wondering, *When is the Messiah going to show Himself?* Satan was saying, "Now is the time! Do it!"

Early in His ministry, Jesus said things like, "My time has not come yet. It's not the time; don't tell anybody" (Mark 8:30, John 2:4, and John 7:6 just to name a few examples). Here Satan was saying, "No, tell them. Go ahead and get this show on the road. Show them You are powerful." Satan was appealing to the human desire for power, but Jesus (because He knew the Scriptures) was able to respond yet again from Deuteronomy—this time Deuteronomy 6:16.

Jesus knew He had nothing to prove to the Enemy in that moment, so He refused. We, however, are constantly building our resume, accessorizing our character in the show called life, trying to one-up somebody, living a constant game of comparison. As long as we're a little bit better than them, we can sleep. Jesus basically says to that: "I don't have to prove anything to you. In a little while, you are going to see an empty tomb. That will be all the evidence you need. I don't have to prove anything to you."

Finally, at the end of the story, everything comes to a head.

> Again, the devil took him to a very high mountain and showed him all the kingdoms of the world and their splendor. "All this I will give you," he said, "if you will bow down and worship me."
>
> Jesus said to him, "Away from me, Satan! For it is written: 'Worship the Lord your God, and serve him only.'"
>
> Then the devil left him, and angels came and attended him. (Matthew 4:8–11)

"I worship the Lord God — only"

Jesus responded with Scripture (again), quoting Deuteronomy 6:13, and essentially told Satan to get lost. It would be easy for us to lose sight of what's happening here. Remember: Satan is called the god of this world and the prince of the air. He has power here on earth. If temptation is a proposition to not trust God, what he was offering Jesus here was a shortcut. He was telling Jesus, "You can have the world. Everything you can see on this earth—my territory—can be yours if you will worship me. And you can skip the whole cross thing." While Satan could only offer Jesus earthly power (and nothing more), it would allow Him to escape earthly suffering. If He would forsake His heavenly Father, the villain would give Him power and let Him skip the cross. Who wouldn't want to skip the cross?!

How much does Jesus love you to say no to that offer? He was saying here, "No, you don't understand. I am willingly dying for them. I love them." The Bible says in Hebrews 12:2, "For the joy set before him he endured the cross." Some of us need to be reminded of that simple truth. He skipped the shortcut and resisted the temptation that so many of us would give in to.

Here's something you must know (and you can test with the Scriptures): You are never going to get away with sin—never. Not one time. It will never happen. No one in the history of the world has every gotten away with sin. But let me say this: You are never going to *have* to sin. Isn't that great news? Never in your life will you think, *Okay, I have two options. One is sin and two is sin.* That will never happen. You'll never have to sin. There is always an option to forgo temptation and follow God's will, regardless of how difficult it is. Paul, in his letter to the church in Corinth, said, "No temptation has overtaken you except what is common to mankind. And God is faithful; he will not let you be tempted beyond what you can bear. But when you are tempted, he will also provide a way out so that you can endure it" (1 Corinthians 10:13). In every situation there is a way out, and you will never be tempted beyond what you can endure.

THERE'S A VERSE FOR THAT

As we fight temptation, it's important to do the same thing Jesus did: use the Word of God. The best way to combat a lie is with the truth. The best way to combat the temptations of the villain is with the truth of God's Word. The villain's tactics are poison, and the truth of God's Word is the antidote. By internalizing and memorizing Scripture, we can pull the verse for the situation we are in. You will be amazed at how the grip of sin loosens when we respond with the truth of Scripture.

Dallas Willard was one of the most well-known authors on the topic of spiritual disciplines. He wrote, "If I had to choose between all the disciplines of the spiritual life, I would choose Bible memorization, because it is a fundamental way of filling our minds with what it needs."[1] When we are presented with an opportunity to sin—to reach for power, to take the shortcut, to click on the hashtag, to lose our temper—we are almost instantaneously reminded of Scripture. It allows us to choose the full life that Jesus offers.

When I became a believer, I became obsessed with learning God's Word. Left to my own devices, I don't love to read. School was always hard for me, and reading was never my thing. But when the Holy Spirit came into my life, I wanted to read and memorize all the Scripture I could because I found it so helpful—and not just helpful but supernaturally relevant to my own life. Then God surrounded me with people who knew His Word. Have you ever known people like that, who are fluent in speaking Scripture?

During that pivotal season, I had friends, bosses, and small group members all around me who seemed to have a verse for every situation. They spoke into my life. When I saw that, I wanted to learn to do the same thing, so I started doing what they did. I spent time reading the Scriptures and I committed verses to memory. I knew it would help in my fight against the Enemy.

RESISTANCE TRAINING

When I moved to Waco, a couple of coworkers and I started the *Becoming Something* podcast. We took the approach of pointing people to the Bible. To simplify the formula and show you our cards, the reason the podcast is helpful to so many people is because we point people to Scripture. As they wage war against sin, we give them the Word. Any topical episode we have ever done is trying to answer the question, What does the Bible say about _____? Pride, lust, greed, anger, alcohol, materialism—whatever the sin issue is—there are verses in Scripture to help.

Have you ever seen someone in the gym bench-press more than any human should? Can you see it? There are like four plates on each side. The bar is bending because of the weight. They seem to effortlessly push it up and down. Here's what you can be certain of: This is not the weight they started with. By utilizing resistance training, they worked up to that amount of weight by pushing against lesser weight and getting stronger. Resistance training means that you push against something that resists you. In doing so, you build muscle. You build strength. You build endurance. This is the way to train yourself for godliness.

As you live as a Christ follower, you will encounter temptations—things you must resist. Temptation to sin never fully goes away. There is no cruise control in Christianity. I must never get to a place where I shift into fifth gear and take it easy. Every day is a fight.

It's important to understand that the more you resist sin, the more you resist sin. Perhaps I am stating the obvious, but to rephrase that sentence: *The more you fight sin, the more you are able to fight against sin.* You build up a resistance to it. This opposition strengthens you. Resistance training strengthens you. You are pushing against something stronger. It's very easy to understand this when you think about muscles—when we press up against the bench, the bench fights back, it resists us, and the muscles break down and grow bigger. Our spiritual growth works the same way. The more we resist, the stronger we become.

MAKE IT STICK: SURROUND YOURSELF WITH TRUTH

As you wage war against sin in your life, it is important to ask yourself a few questions.

First, what are the areas in your life where the villain wants to tempt you the most? How would the Enemy take you out if you gave him a foothold? Maybe it's lust, control, pride, or the fear of man. Write down all the areas where you feel susceptible.

Second, what scriptures should you commit to memory? What verses do you need to know so the next time you are tempted, you can respond with the Word of God?

Here's my challenge to you: Spend some time with your Bible today and find those verses. Write them on sticky notes. Make them the background on your phone. Post them in your car. Put the words of Scripture to a familiar tune so you can sing the truth over and over. Put the truth wherever you are going, so you see it often. Don't remove them until each scripture is committed to memory.

CHAPTER 13

GUARDING YOUR HEART

MY WIFE IS AMAZING AT DIRECTIONS. YOU COULD blindfold Monica, drop her off somewhere, and she could find her way home. Me? Not so much.

If you have ever ridden in a car with me, you know how bad I am with directions. Because of that fact, I was an early adopter of in-car GPS systems. A couple of years ago I got a new car (technically a used car that was new to me), and I was making the ninety-mile drive south back home to Waco from Dallas Fort Worth International Airport, just outside of Dallas proper. This car had the feature where you could just hit "home" on the navigation screen and the GPS would direct you to your saved address. Eager to get home, I got in the car, hit the "home" button, and started my drive.

Now, I have made this drive dozens of times. Hundreds maybe. First, it sent me to Dallas, which I thought was weird because that seemed too far east when I was trying to get south. But I was thinking, *Okay, no problem. It must sense there is traffic—it's smart like that.* And so I drove over to Dallas from the airport. Then it sent me all the way through Dallas. Again, odd. Now I was east of Dallas, thinking, *This feels interesting, but it's smarter than me.* Listen, I have challenged the GPS many times, and I have lost every time. I wasn't trying to prove a point. So I was just determined to do what it said. Then it had me start driving north, which was weird because our house is very much south of Dallas.

Driving down the road, I was having a conversation in my head, trying to figure out what was going on. It was late and I just wanted to get home and go to sleep. Then I realized that somehow it had reverted to the previous car owner's home address. I don't know how that happened, but it was taking me to his house, way up in the northern suburbs of Dallas.

Before following the navigation system's instructions, I had to input the right destination. Your heart works the same way. Far too many people follow their hearts before they input their destination. Before you listen to your heart and before you follow it, you must inform it, and you must set it on the right course. You see, our hearts guide us way more than we think they do.

Even the most logical, rational person reading this is driven by their heart more than they realize. What's the difference between the mind and the heart? We're speaking in metaphors here, because we are not talking about the organ that pumps blood. Simply put, your mind is your thoughts and your heart is your feelings. Your mind feeds your heart, and then Scripture says everything we do flows from that (Proverbs 4:23).

The Enemy is after your heart, just like he and his forces are after your mind and your thoughts. This chapter goes hand in hand with the chapter on desensitization, because the things we take in and feed our hearts ultimately drive our actions when we operate out of our emotions. What we put into our minds eventually informs our hearts, then what goes into our hearts determines what comes out of our lives. If we feed our minds evil things, that feeds our hearts. If our hearts are filled with evil, our outlook is more inclined to do evil, think evil, speak evil, and be evil. We do wrong and hurtful things. Knowing this, why wouldn't we want to build a fortress around our hearts?

WHAT IT MEANS TO GUARD YOUR HEART

The first nine chapters of Proverbs really consist of ten lectures. It is as if a father is speaking to his son, giving him wisdom he needs to succeed in life.

In Proverbs 4, Solomon was writing out another lecture about where and how to gain wisdom. As a reminder, Solomon was the wisest man to ever live (with the exception of Jesus), as well as the wealthiest person to have ever lived. This lecture reads almost like a pep talk, almost like Coach Solomon is clapping his hands and imploring his audience to stay focused and listen to what he has to say. Here is what he said:

> My son, pay attention to what I say;
>   turn your ear to my words.
> Do not let them out of your sight,
>   keep them within your heart;
> for they are life to those who find them
>   and health to one's whole body.
> Above all else, guard your heart,
>   for everything you do flows from it.
> Keep your mouth free of perversity;
>   keep corrupt talk far from your lips.

Let your eyes look straight ahead;
       fix your gaze directly before you.
Give careful thought to the paths for your feet
       and be steadfast in all your ways.
Do not turn to the right or the left;
       keep your foot from evil. (Proverbs 4:20–27)

Now, if you have spent any significant amount of time in the church, you have probably heard Proverbs 4:23 and the instruction to "guard your heart." It feels like this verse has been hijacked and reserved for the fifteen-year-old girl at church camp. She leaves just as confused as all of you are, because someone like me is up on a stage saying, "You need to guard your heart." She's thinking, *Okay, what does that mean?*

This verse is just as relevant for the seventy-year-old as the fifteen-year-old. It is just as relevant for men as it is women, husbands and wives, fathers and mothers, single people, young adults, senior adults, and high school students. When Solomon wrote this, he was not thinking about the girl at church camp or the couple that has been dating for six weeks. That's not who he was talking to. It can be relevant there, but it means more than the narrow definition it has taken on.

The Enemy loves the unguarded heart because it means you are at your most willing to follow his lead. So, what does it mean to guard your heart? It means that you and I need to be very careful what we allow in. Do we think about this enough? The term Solomon used here when talking about "guarding" is a military term. It's the way that a guard would protect a castle: with violence, hostility, vigilance, alertness, awareness, and a strategy. A guard with that kind of mindset is saying, "No one is going to come into this castle. I must protect it." The instruction here is to *above all else* guard your heart in that same manner.

Think about that—*above all else*. More than you protect your children, more than you protect your home with a security system, more than you protect yourself in your five-star-safety-rated SUV, and more than you protect your money with FDIC insurance. More than we protect anything else we are to guard our hearts. And why do we need to guard our hearts? Because the heart is going to seek what you feed it. It's a very simple idea that you could spend hours and hours meditating and journaling on.

Based on this passage from Proverbs 4, I see five questions that each one of us needs to answer as we think through how to guard our hearts. Each of these questions is meant to give you more tools in your toolbelt as you look for ways to fight back against the tactics of the Enemy. If the villain is prowling around and looking for someone to devour, you'd better believe he wants to devour the one whose heart is unprotected.

1. Who Am I Listening To?

Who gets to inform what your heart holds on to? A challenge in life, from the time you are a small child until you breathe your last breath, is that you have to choose who you will and will not listen to. Notice what Solomon said: "My son, pay attention to what I say; turn your ear to my words. Do not let them out of your sight, keep them within your heart" (vv. 20–21). That plays out practically in something called *feedback bias*. When we feel a particular way, we look for people who feel that way also.

Put another way, misery loves company. But company doesn't have to be an actual person. If I feel a particular way, I want to read a book by someone who feels that way, I want to listen to someone who feels that way, and I'm looking for somebody to agree with me, which feeds and grows my emotions.

This happens with the music we listen to, the podcasts we consume, and the people we associate with at work. The Enemy is so crafty that with a beat behind it or some jokes thrown in, he can fill our minds with the exact opposite of the truth of the gospel. We can consume things that defile the heart and turn us in a different direction.

Think about how often we are entertained by stories about others. Gossip is a tool of the Enemy; I am so convinced of that. Proverbs 18:8 says that gossip is like "choice morsels." We love to hear it because it makes us feel better about ourselves. It turns our hearts against other people made in the image of God, and it's another way the Enemy can distract and divide us against one another. How do we combat that? We cut it off at the beginning. We protect what we hear. As soon as the conversation pivots to somebody not present, we shut it down and suggest to the person speaking that they need to talk *to* the person they are referencing, not *about* them. We make ourselves an unsafe place for gossip, because that will protect our heart and theirs. Because who (and what) we listen to affects our hearts.

2. What Am I Saying?

The next question is, What is coming out of your own mouth? What are you saying? Proverbs 4:24 says, "Keep your mouth free of perversity; keep corrupt talk far from your lips." You might be arguing with me in your head, thinking, *Does what I say really impact my heart?* It absolutely does. Maybe more than just about anything else and, according to Jesus, it certainly displays what is in your heart.

Jesus, while He was here on earth, said in Matthew 15:18–20, "The things that come out of a person's mouth come from the heart, and these defile them. For out of the heart come evil thoughts—murder, adultery, sexual immorality, theft, false testimony, slander. These are what defile a person." What comes out of your mouth is indicative of what is in your heart. Scripture speaks over and over about the power of the tongue. James (the half-brother of Jesus) even compared it to a fire (James 3:6)! Why? Because words have power and meaning. The Enemy can use flippant speech to drive wedges between believers, split apart marriages, and squash movements of God.

In his letter to the church in Ephesus, Paul gave us an amazingly simple test to know if our speech is helpful or not. It is basically a pass-fail test. He wrote, "Do not let any unwholesome talk come out of your mouths, but only what is helpful for building others up . . . that it may benefit those who listen" (Ephesians 4:29). Is it unwholesome? Then don't say it. Does it build others up? If yes, say it and encourage people. Does it cut them down? Then don't say it. As a parent, I have had that conversation with my kids over and over. But it is not like we graduate from that ourselves.

How do you speak about your spouse? Is there ever a scenario, in all of creation, where you should ever say something negative about your spouse? I am here to tell you that speaking negatively about your spouse will not grow your heart for them. If you are in a covenant relationship and you say something negative about them, it is not going to grow your heart for them, which means your marriage just got more difficult. "Just venting with the boys" or "It was just girls' night" is not a good excuse. That kind of talk is not of God; it is selfish and worldly and it will chip away at the covenant you have made. The villain of your life is after your marriage, even if you haven't met your spouse yet! The pure in heart only speak what builds others up.

3. Where Am I Looking for Guidance?

Where do your eyes go? Where are you looking for guidance, information, and entertainment? Solomon said in Proverbs 4:25, "Let your eyes look straight ahead; fix your gaze directly before you." I've heard it said that far too often we are entertained by the things that Christ died for. Whatever you consume, it feeds and grows your preferences. Sometimes it seems harmless, but a lot of it breeds discontentment in your heart. You watch shows about fixing up old houses and then you grow discontent in your house. You watch *Shark Tank* and you decide you hate your job and you would rather be your own boss and create your own product (and I *love Shark Tank*). What you watch stirs up something in your heart, causing you to look elsewhere, and the Enemy loves when your eyes wander away from the message of the gospel.

Sometimes where you are looking is not so harmless. Sometimes it takes you places you do not want to go. We love a good whodunit. What did they do and where and why? *Forensic Files, Dateline NBC, Snapped, Serial,* true crime . . . all these things are so popular right now. I heard a story recently where a guy went from being obsessed with true-crime shows and then eventually ended up committing the same crimes from the shows he compulsively watched. Now, he didn't get there overnight. But no one does.

Your heart is like a smartphone. It hears what you are interested in (surely, I am not the only one whose phone is listening to them), and it begins to put it in front of you. If I tell Monica we need a new rug, suddenly everywhere I look online there are rug ads. It knows I am looking for rugs and it starts feeding me rugs. That is how your heart works! It sees what you take an interest in, and it begins to place it in front of you. Social media is the worst for this. Here's what social media has taught me recently: All your lives are so much better than mine. You guys go places and do stuff, and I was at home doing nothing. You go skiing and to the beach and you're always exploring new cities!

What am I doing? I'm feeding discontentment. It is self-harm. We start playing the comparison game and we compare ourselves to the best mom we know, the influencer who seems to have it all, or the person who seems to never have a bad day. The villain wants you to play the comparison game. He wants you to get caught up in a true-crime show or anything else that will pull you away from the Great Commission that Jesus has given us. Any distraction will work for him. The pure in heart will set no evil or unholy thing before their eyes (Psalm 101:3). I know that feels like strong language. The admonition to guard our hearts is even stronger. This really matters to God because He doesn't want His children to stray toward things that will bring them pain.

4. When Do I Plan My Path?

Solomon said this in Proverbs 4:26: "Give careful thought to the paths for your feet and be steadfast in all your ways." When, how often, and at what time do you plan out your path and where you want to go? This proverb is saying that you can't be steadfast without being thoughtful, and being thoughtful requires setting time aside to think. By planning your path, I mean how do we ensure we are steadily going the right direction? And how do we spend daily time with Jesus and prioritize consuming God's Word?

We talked about Satan's tactic of distraction earlier in the book. So many of us are living such hurried, distracted, hectic lives that we don't set aside the time needed to be thoughtful about *how* we are going to follow Jesus. We rush from place to place, event to event, meeting to meeting, and practice to practice, and we hope to make it to church *most* Sundays out of the month. Compare that to the description of the church in Acts 2 where they gathered daily and shared meals together. To fight back against what modern Christianity has settled for as "normal," we must be willing to press pause, invite others in, and be *thoughtful.*

For years, I have been giving the same advice: If you are on the wrong path, change your playmates and your playground. Change who you hang out with and where you go for fun. Hang out with people on the right path who are going the right direction. Nothing has sharpened me more than sitting in living rooms with small groups of other believers over the past couple of decades, learning from them and allowing them to speak into my life.

Eugene Peterson wrote, "Scripture knows nothing of the solitary Christian."[1] Think about it: From the very inception of Christianity, it was always a communal effort. Christians are meant to live alongside one another—quirks and all—to spur each other on to love and follow Jesus more (Hebrews 10:24). Do not try to do this alone. Lock arms and push back the kingdom of darkness together.

5. What Causes Me to Stray?

What causes you to stray? This is another way of asking the same question from the beginning of the book: How would the Enemy take you out? What are the tendencies you turn toward? What are the temptations that you, left to your own devices, would return to? This is a question I ask often because it reveals a lot about our own self-awareness. If something is evil, stay far from it. Do not poke it, do not sniff it, do not taste it. Run from it, and stay away from it.

Imagine you are alone in a room. As you look at the four walls of the room, you see the walls are lined with doors. All the doors are shut, but they all represent paths to sin. Over the doors are signs with specific sins like materialism, pornography, greed, envy, drunkenness, and addiction. Behind each door is a lion that desires to devour you. When you sin, you unlock that door. When you sin again, you turn the knob. When you sin again, you leave the door open. When you sin again, you open it wider. If you keep sinning, pretty soon there is not even a door there anymore. The villain can devour you anytime he wants.

Lust, pornography, and sexual addiction are a part of my past.

That's a part of my journey to Jesus. And because of my past, I feel like most days I'm still fighting. I know at any given moment I am a few clicks away from wrecking everything. If there is a door and Satan is on the other side of that door, I feel like I have my back against the door, holding it shut with all my strength. I padlock it, put a chain on it, put a bar on the door, and do everything I can to hold it shut.

In verse 27 of Proverbs 4, Solomon wrote, "Do not turn to the right or to the left; keep your foot from evil." Keep your back against the door.

A couple of years ago, somebody recommended that I watch a show called *Reacher*. The way they described it, it sounded great. I failed to research it before I started it, so as I was watching the show, a strip club scene with topless dancers came on for about three seconds. In that short amount of time, it felt like I walked over to that door, removed the chain, undid the deadlock, removed the bar, turned the knob, and cracked it open. I felt like I was now walking around waiting to be devoured.

Because of those three seconds, I felt a greater inclination to sin in that way. After that three-second TV scene, I felt like I could not be trusted with Instagram. And this is embarrassing to say because I'm a pastor. I can't go to the Explore page because the villain is there waiting to trap me.

Not everyone has the same Instagram Explore page temptation as me. Some people struggle with comparison or shame or materialism. They go to their Instagram Explore page and feed the mom guilt or the desire to buy a new car. So it grows. Meanwhile, some demonic stronghold or force is pleased because he has you right where he wants you. That is actively happening every day.

You might read all this and say, "I get the point you're trying to make, but this all sounds too legalistic." Listen, if you are ever going to be legalistic about anything, let it be in the way that you guard your heart. Remember what the Bible says at the beginning of Proverbs 4:23? Above all else, guard your heart! If you are a parent, protect your kids' hearts. Protect them at all costs.

MAKE IT STICK: FIVE QUESTIONS

Think back on the five questions asked in this chapter. Set aside some time to answer each question thoughtfully and honestly.

Once you've done that, reflect: What in your life needs to change so you can build a fortress around your heart?

What am I listening to?
Saying?
Where am I looking for guidance?
When do I plan my path?
What causes me to stray?

2/11/25 SNOW DAY

CONCLUSION

Loosening the Villain's Grip

A WHILE BACK, I SPOKE AT AN EVENT WITH THE leading exorcist for the Roman Catholic Church. (I know that is kind of a surprising sentence, so feel free to reread it if you need to.) It is literally his job to train priests on how to perform exorcisms. I didn't even know that was a job! The day before we met, he had performed three exorcisms. Just a normal workday for him.

The event was filled with people from all across the spectrum of Christianity, and the speakers would discuss different hot topics for ten to fifteen minutes. While listening to his talk, I was fascinated by what he was saying. I knew I wanted to talk to him more. Later on, I had the chance to pepper him with questions. I was so encouraged by his humility and the beliefs that we share about Jesus and the Enemy.

While he was talking, he said something that really stuck with me—and I have been thinking about it ever since. It is something we all know to be true in a "nod our heads" kind of way, but I am not convinced it has fully sunk into all of our hearts. We all believe that the Bible teaches that when we sin, we are inviting Satan in. We are giving him a foothold. We are opening ourselves up to the Enemy. We can all agree that is a biblical concept. We've even discussed it multiple times throughout this book. But, he noted, we can often find ourselves living in this paradoxical way where we will pray one moment and say, "God, please protect my family, keep my children safe, and bless my marriage," and the next moment we go look at porn, go drink too much, or go make another impulse purchase.

Do you see how confusing that is? That must frustrate God as He is watching us in real time. You are inviting the Enemy to set up shop and build a home in your heart every time that happens. You know that your story has a villain. Why would you invite him in?

The longer I follow Jesus, the more I am convinced: To live the full, abundant life that Jesus offers us, we must be committed to the long, bumpy, and often difficult road of faithfulness.

Friends, you will never achieve perfection. You will never reach a sinless existence. You will continue to stub your toes, fall on your faces, and return to sin that you do not want to do, only to repent and turn back and start walking the road of faithfulness once again. Christian maturity is not an overnight process, as much as we may want it to be. While the Enemy would love for that to discourage you, the Scriptures actually tell us to *expect* it. But we cannot lose heart; we must keep fighting.

FINISHING THE RACE

An often-used metaphor in the New Testament to describe the Christian life is a long race—finish line and all. Paul returned to it multiple times in multiple letters written to both churches and individuals. The author of Hebrews instructed us to "run with perseverance the race marked out for us, fixing our eyes on Jesus, the pioneer and perfecter of faith" (Hebrews 12:1–2). There is no mystery here. We should expect a long road ahead of us.

One of my daughters ran cross-country for her school. I have no idea why she signed up for it. I always thought Monica and I raised her better (keep in mind, I don't even like to run errands), but it was her choice, so we went along with it. When I went to her first meet, I wasn't quite sure what to expect. I knew there would be running through bumpy terrain, but that was it. When the runners showed up, people were there to help them. They understood the course and it was their job to walk the runners through the course and show them the way to go.

By the time I showed up, the runners had already taken off, so I was just standing there in a field with a lot of people waiting for a racer to show up. After a little time passed, suddenly I looked to my right and there was a girl running toward me, then another one, and then another one.

Now, I am not a guy who never cries, but I am also not usually a guy who cries at middle school cross-country races (I usually only cry when I run, not when other people do). Watching them all come through the trees and running toward the finish line, I had an emotional response. I could see them pushing through, one foot after the other, knowing full well how agonizing of a race it was by the looks on their faces.

Standing there, everyone in the crowd watched them as they made their way around the field, and then to the finish line: a ribbon that they would run through, and a rope on each side holding the spectators out of the raceway. I saw these girls giving it their all, running their hearts out. Everyone in the crowd was cheering them on, saying, "You can do it! You can do it!" As they crossed that finish line, they collapsed to the ground, struggling to catch their breath.

Eventually, they got up. They came over to the side of the

rope and joined in the cheering crowd with any ounce of energy they had left, yelling, "Come on! You can do it! Come on! You're almost there! You can finish! Come on! I know you can!" They were cheering on their teammates and fellow runners. Standing there, I thought, *What a picture of what the church is to be.*

As we run our race, and run our race to the end, we are going to fall across that finish line. Exhausted. But we have brothers and sisters who have gone before us, cheering, "Come on! You can do it! Stay in the race! Don't give up! Don't give up hope! Yeah, the Enemy is crafty. But don't quit! You can finish! You can do it! It's worth it!"

After the race, we gathered Finley's things as the crowd dispersed. People started going home, thinking the race was over. We started walking to my truck. We were halfway to the parking lot when I saw one girl by herself make the corner and head toward the finish line by herself.

She was the last runner. I said, "Hey, we need to go back."

We split up as we got closer to the finish line. I went to one side and Finley went to the other. As loud as we could we cheered and shouted, "Keep going! You can do it! Keep going! You're almost there!" That girl crossed that finish line, and one of her family members threw their arms around her, and said, "I'm so proud of you for finishing!" And it dawned on me, in the kingdom, she has the same inheritance as the person who finished first. They both get heaven. They both get eternity in paradise. She gets the same kingdom that the girl with the first-place medal gets. And it is all worth it.

SHARE YOUR STORY

As you pursue the road of faithfulness, you get to be one of the ones cheering along everyone else running the race. How do you do that? You use the story God has given you. Deep inside of me is a conviction that every time you tell your story, the Enemy's grip on your life loosens a little bit more, then a little bit more, then a little bit more. The more you tell your story over time, the less of a hold the Enemy has on your heart. I know for some of you, it's very difficult to say words like *abuse, abandonment, rape, neglect, divorce*, and so on. But you can do this! You can tell your story and run your race toward a good end, no matter what happened along the way.

Time and time again in my own life, I have seen God do this exact thing: use people's stories. By this point in the book, you know a lot of my story. I am a chump from a small town in Texas who grew up in the church, then chased after everything the world had to offer. I was addicted to pornography, gripped by alcohol, and self-absorbed, living as if I was the center of the world. Then, as I was sitting in the back row of a church, hungover from the night before, God grabbed ahold of my heart in a whole new way.

People have said to me before, "Why do you tell your story all the time, JP? You are always up there talking about pornography and alcohol and the party scene and this and that. Why do you do that?" Because we are supposed to. Maybe your story is different and that was not your thing. Maybe you were saved at a young age and don't remember a time you didn't trust Jesus. Awesome. What's the struggle you are tempted with by the villain? Is it self-righteousness? Is it pride? How can you turn that into a story God uses to set someone free?

Trust me, I have so many regrets from my life before Christ. I wish I could have so many do-overs. But at the same time, I feel total freedom. For as long as I can remember, God has made me extremely comfortable in telling my story, because if He can use me, He can use anybody. I try to tell my church often that there is nothing in my head, heart, or past that I would not share with them. If I lived in shame and guilt and kept that story to myself, it wouldn't help anybody else find freedom.

The Enemy loves when we keep our stories to ourselves because it keeps others chained up.

Do you remember the story of the demon-possessed man in chapter three? You know, the one where Jesus went across the lake and cast the demons out of the man and then they went into the pigs? The end of that story is really interesting and worth revisiting. This entire scene became a spectacle. Some people were terrified. Everyone was talking about it.

The guy, who was notorious around town, was clothed, in his right mind, and was sitting right next to Jesus. As the chatter picked up, Jesus went to leave, and when the guy wanted to go with him, Jesus told him no. Why? Because Jesus wanted this guy to tell everyone what He had done. So, He told him to return home and do just that.

Jesus used that man, with that message, to tell everyone around him what had happened. From that moment, you see the gospel burst forth. This guy was a Gentile, and the good news of Jesus spread like crazy through Gentile territory. He told somebody, who told somebody, who told somebody, and so on and so on. And then one day, somebody told *you*. That's how this works.

God flips the script and uses the story of a formerly possessed, enslaved, chained-up outcast of a man to tell everyone what Jesus does.

You have a story, and it has a villain. But you also have a Savior who wins every time. Share your story of victory and help set others free.

EPILOGUE

A Villain's Reply

JANUARY 16, 2025

Dear Molech,

With a heavy heart and seething frustration, I must report a lamentable turn in our once promising strategy. Our grand design, architected by Lucifer himself, to wield the pandemic as a weapon of division, has encountered an unforeseen and deeply vexing obstacle.

Contrary to our expectations, the very crisis we hoped would tear them asunder is, infuriatingly, uniting them. Where we anticipated discord, there bursts a spirit of unity; where we sowed doubt, somehow faith has taken root stronger than before. Our efforts to exploit their fears have backfired in a most disheartening manner.

Take the case of the human, David, whom we thought we would crush by grief and despair. The passing of his father, a scenario ripe for engendering bitterness, has instead kindled a flame of compassion and solidarity within him. He has become a beacon of hope and a source of empathy, frustratingly drawing others into a circle of care and support.

Church doors, which we hoped would remain closed, have instead opened wider. The Christians, rather than cowering in fear and suspicion, are banding together. They're not only returning to their churches but are also spilling out into their communities with acts of kindness, care, and an infuriating resolve to help one another. I hate to report that we forced them to innovate, and that technology is now being used to reach people beyond their walls.

Their conversations with their Maker, rather than diminishing, have intensified in fervor and frequency. It's as if each challenge we orchestrate only serves to deepen their faith, drawing them closer to their Creator rather than driving them away.

It is a bitter pill to swallow, Molech! I am confident in Lucifer's disgust. Our tactics, it seems, have only served to fortify their resolve and unity. We must regroup and rethink our strategy, for our current path leads only to failure and the strengthening of their bond with the One we oppose.

In shared frustration,

Abaddon

√Zoom
√ tele
√ calls
meetings

NOTES

FOREWORD
1. Henna Inam, "Leadership and the Boiling Frog Experiment." Forbes, August 29, 2013. https://www.forbes.com/sites /hennainam/2013/08/28/leadership-and-the-boiling -frog-experiment/.
2. Paul A. Hartog, "Drunkenness," ed. Douglas Mangum et al., Lexham Theological Wordbook, Lexham Bible Reference Series (Lexham Press, 2014).
3. P. J. Budd, "Νήφω," ed. Lothar Coenen, Erich Beyreuther, and Hans Bietenhard, New International Dictionary of New Testament Theology (Zondervan Publishing House, 1986), 514.

INTRODUCTION
1. Wade Goodwyn, "Waco Recalls 90-Year-Old 'Horror,'" *All Things Considered*, National Public Radio, May 13, 2006, https://www. npr.org/2006/05/13/5401868/waco-recalls-a-90-year-old-horror.

CHAPTER 1
1. Ligonier Ministires and Lifeway Research, "The State of Theology," accessed May 30, 2024, https://thestateoftheology.com /data-explorer/2022/20?AGE=30&MF=14&REGION=30&DENSIT Y=62&EDUCATION=62&INCOME=254&MARITAL=126&ETH NICITY=62&RELTRAD=62&EVB=6&ATTENDANCE=254.

2. Bible Project, "Vocab Insight: Gehenna/ Valley of Wailing," BibleProject.com, April 22, 2024, https://bibleproject.com/explore /video/vocab-insight-gehenna-valley-wailing/#:~:text=The%20 New%20Testament%20Greek%20word,the%20southwest%20 side%20of%20Jerusalem.

3. Eminem, "'97 Bonnie & Clyde," *The Slim Shady LP,* 1999, Aftermath Entertainment and Interscope Records.

CHAPTER 2

1. C. S. Lewis, *Screwtape Letters* (HarperOne, 2001), ix.

2. Got Questions Ministries, "Was Satan in Charge of Music in Heaven?," GotQuestions.com, November 14, 2022, https://www.gotquestions.org/Satan-music.html.

CHAPTER 3

1. Got Questions Ministries, "Where Do Demons Come From?," GotQuestions.com, January 4, 2022, https://www.gotquestions .org/where-do-demons-come-from.html.

2. Matthew 8:28–9:1; Mark 5:1–20; Luke 8:26–39.

3. Timothy Keller, "The Defeat of Evil," *Gospel in Life*, podcast, April 27, 2022, https://podcast.gospelinlife.com/e/the-defeat-of-evil/.

PART 2

1. Tara Brach, "Nourishing Heartwood," *Psychology Today,* August 6, 2018, https://www.psychologytoday.com/us/blog /finding-true-refuge/201808/nourishing-heartwood.

CHAPTER 4

1. Carol J. Williams, "Haitians Hail the 'President of Voodoo,'" *LA Times*, August 3, 2003, https://www.latimes.com/archives /la-xpm-2003-aug-03-fg-voodoo3-story.html.

2. Richard Pallardy, "2010 Haiti earthquake," *Britannica,* updated June 18, 2024, https://www.britannica.com /event/2010-Haiti-earthquake#:~:text=Figures%20released%20

by%20Haitian%20government,hundred%20thousand%20
more%20had%20perished.

CHAPTER 5

1. John Piper (@JohnPiper), "One of the great uses . . . ,"
   Twitter (X), October 20, 2009, https://twitter.com
   /JohnPiper/status/5027319857.
2. Richard Foster, *Celebration of Discipline* (HarperOne, 2018), 15.
3. Juan R. Sanchez, *First Peter For You* (The Good Book Company,
   2016), 46.
4. "A Brief History of the Benedictine Order," OSB.org, accessed
   June 3, 2024, https://osb.org/our-roots/a-brief-history
   -of-the-benedictine-order/.

CHAPTER 7

1. World Health Organization, "COVID-19 Pandemic Triggers 25%
   Increase in Prevalence of Anxiety and Depression Worldwide,"
   WHO.int, March 2, 2022, https://www.who.int/news/item
   /02–03–2022-covid-19-pandemic-triggers-25-increase-in
   -prevalence-of-anxiety-and-depression-worldwide.
2. Kat Devlin, Moira Fagan, and Aidan Connaughton, "People in
   Advanced Economies Say Their Society Is More Divided Than
   Before Pandemic," Pew Research Center, June 23, 2021,
   https://www.pewresearch.org/global/2021/06/23/people-in
   -advanced-economies-say-their-society-is-more-divided-than
   -before-pandemic/.
3. Centers for Disease Control, "Adolescent Behaviors and
   Experiences Survey—United States, January–June 2021,"
   Supplements 71, no. 3 (April 1, 2022), cited in Tina Reed
   and Adriel Bettelheim, "American teens' health behaviors
   suffered a lot during the pandemic," *Axios*, April 3, 2022,
   https://www.axios.com/2022/04/01/american-teens-health
   -behaviors-suffered-a-lot-during-pandemic.

4. Peter Beinart, "Breaking Faith," *Atlantic,* April 2017, https://www.theatlantic.com/magazine/archive/2017/04 /breaking-faith/517785/.

5. Eugene Peterson, *The Jesus Way* (Wm. B. Eerdmans, 2007), 230.

CHAPTER 8

1. Council on Communications and Media, "Media Violence," *Pediatrics* 124, no. 5 (November 2009): 1495–1503.

2. *Nefarious,* directed by Chuck Konzelman and Cary Solomon (Believe Entertainment, 2023).

3. Timothy Keller, *Counterfeit Gods* (Hodder & Stoughton, 2010), 24.

CHAPTER 9

1. Barna Group, "Atheism Doubles Among Generation Z," Barna.com, January 24, 2018, https://www.barna.com/research /atheism-doubles-among-generation-z/.

CHAPTER 10

1. Charles Baily, ed., "Commentary on Ephesians 6:16," *Contending for the Faith,* studylight.org, accessed July 12, 2024, https://www.studylight.org/commentaries/ctf/ephesians-6.html.

2. David Van Biema, "Mother Teresa's Crisis of Faith," *Time,* August 23, 2007, https://time.com/4126238/mother-teresas-crisis -of-faith/; C. S. Lewis, *A Grief Observed* (HarperCollins, 1989); Diana Gruver, "Charles Spurgeon Knew It Was Possible to Be Faithful and Depressed," *Christianity Today,* February 26, 2021, https://www.christianitytoday.com/ct/2021/february-web-only /diana-gruver-companions-darkness-spurgeon-depression.html.

3. Ryan Griffith, "Martin Luther's Shelter Amid the Flood of Depression," The Gospel Coalition, July 6, 2017, https://www.thegospelcoalition.org/article/martin-luthers -shelter-amid-flood-of-depression/.

CHAPTER 11

1. Tithely, "How Many Times Is Prayer Mentioned in the Bible?" Tithely.com, accessed June 4, 2024, https://get.tithe.ly/blog /how-many-times-is-prayer-mentioned-in-the-bible.

2. John Piper, "Corporate Prayer in the Life of the Church and in Worship," April 18, 1990, published in *Desiring God* blog, https://www.desiringgod.org/messages/corporate-prayer-in-the -life-of-the-church-and-in-worship.

3. Dan Southerland, *Chair Time* (Journey Ministry, Inc., 2013).

4. Richard Foster, *Celebration of Discipline* (HarperOne, 2018), 37.

CHAPTER 12

1. Dallas Willard, "Spiritual Formation in Christ for the Whole Life and Whole Person," *Vocatio* 12, no. 2 (2001): 7.

CHAPTER 13

1. Eugene Peterson, *A Long Obedience in the Same Direction* (InterVarsity Press, 2000), 170.

ABOUT THE AUTHORS

JONATHAN "JP" POKLUDA IS THE LEAD PASTOR OF Harris Creek Baptist Church and host of the *Becoming Something* podcast. His previous bestselling books include *Why Do I Do What I Don't Want to Do?*, *Outdated*, and *Welcome to Adulting*, as well as the *Welcome to Adulting Survival Guide* and *Welcoming the Future Church*. JP's partner in ministry is Monica, his wife of twenty years, and together they disciple their children Presley, Finley, and Weston.

JON GREEN HAS BEEN ON STAFF AT HARRIS CREEK in Waco, Texas, since 2013. He is a graduate of Baylor University and is the managing editor of BibleReadingPlan.org, a daily devotional and Bible study. Jon and his wife, Amanda, have three young children.

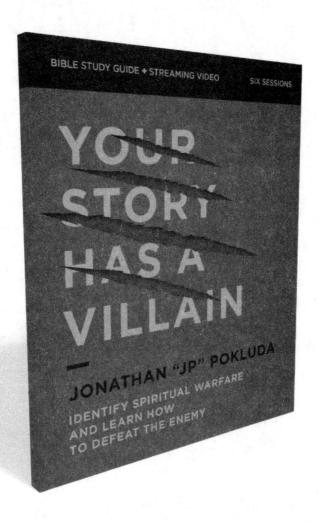
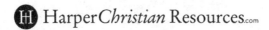